Tranquil Homes

How to Nurture Our Homes as a mainstay of Serenity

Translation of

Deliberations and Intricacies regarding *Tarbiyyah* (Nurturing) of Homes and the Risks that Threaten Them

Dr. Sulaiman Hamd Al-Odah

Translated by
Irfan Padder

Reviewed & Edited by
Fadhl Hasan

Afaq Al Marefa

Dar Ul Thaqafah

First Edition Published by **Afaq Al Marefa**

www.afaqbooks.com

English Edition Published by **Dar Ul Thaqafah**

www.darulthaqafah.com
www.twitter.com/darulthaqafah

A Subsidiary of **MaktabaIslamia Publications**

www.maktabaislamia.com

Contents

Foreword

This book (**Tranquil Homes: How to Nurture Our Homes as a mainstay of Serenity** - Deliberations around developing and upbringing families, and the challenges they face) observes more than one method and mechanism for *Tarbiyyah* (Nurturing) of children. The book also marked specific threats to homes and explained the effects and fruits of *Tarbiyyah* (Nurturing).

The book does not target a particular segment. It is directed to every person keen on *Tarbiyyah* (Nurturing) and making *Islah* (reform) in their homes, and taking the path of betterment.

This book is a practical step towards Islah (reform) and optimal investment in homes and Children. It overcomes blaming each other, and sadness, defeats enemies' plans to spoil Muslim homes, is concerned with fruitful work and setting the path, and considering homes and undertaking *Tarbiyyah* (Nurturing) in them (projects) worthy of consideration and work.

The book's aim is not just to culture but also to benefit from what the reader accepts and agrees with the methods and mechanisms of *Tarbiyyah* (Nurturing). If the reader finds other ways and means of *Tarbiyyah* (Nurturing) that are not mentioned (in this book), then the field is welcoming, and the goal is one (i.e., to reform).

It is enough for the book to trigger (the desire for) taking care of homes, undertaking *Tarbiyyah* (Nurturing) of their inhabitants, being alert of the dangers surrounding them, and how to face them and get rid of them.

This book is not the only effort in its field; rather, it is a participation and an attempt to compile texts in the field of *Tarbiyyah* (Nurturing) while discussing the old and new experiences in the *Tarbiyyah* (Nurturing) of homes. This might not be suitable for an optimal application; however, it is as much as we could so that no one can excuse himself from making *Islah* (reform) in his home and *Tarbiyyah* (Nurturing) his family and his Children.

I pray to Allah (swt) that He (swt) make its benefits reach all, reward those who wrote it, read it, and practice *Tarbiyyah* (Nurturing) in his home for his family and children. I also pray that He (swt) save us, our lands, and all Muslims from every ordeal and mishap.

Dr. SulaIman bin Hamd Al-Odah
Al-Qassim / Buraidah 1441H
Mob: 505143491

Preface

Why the Discussion About Homes

Homes are a place to rest, comfort, and tranquility

$$﴿وَٱللَّهُ جَعَلَ لَكُم مِّنْ بُيُوتِكُمْ سَكَنًا ..﴾﴿٨٠﴾$$

"And Allah (swt) has made your homes a place to rest "–

[TMQ Al-Nahl 80]

They are the first centres where *Tarbiyyah* (Nurturing) is undertaken, the starting point of *Islah* (reform), and the primary fortress; the incubator for the family, the flag bearer and mantle of the Islamic community; whose structures have weakened in other communities.

No matter how much discussion is undertaken and the multitude of books written about homes and the family, the need for more and the diversity in the offering will remain as long as negligence and carelessness will keep taking place in our homes.

There are plenty of reasons for talking about homes, of which I mention the following:

1. In response to the call of the Lord, the blessed and the exalted, to protect (ourselves) from the punishment

$$\text{﴿يَٰٓأَيُّهَا ٱلَّذِينَ ءَامَنُوا۟ قُوٓا۟ أَنفُسَكُمْ وَأَهْلِيكُمْ نَارًا وَقُودُهَا ٱلنَّاسُ وَٱلْحِجَارَةُ ..﴾ ﴿٦﴾}$$

"O believers! Protect yourselves and your families from a Fire whose fuel is people and stones"　　　　[TMQ At-Tahrim 6]

The protection would only be achieved by urging the family and the offspring to obey Allah (swt) and avoid *Maharim* (the forbidden things and acts). All these could be made available by educating and guiding homes, by a sense of responsibility and being in charge

كلكم راعٍ وكلكم مسؤول عن رعيته

Each of you is a shepherd, and each of you is responsible for his flock[1],

إن الله سائل كل راعٍ عما استرعاه أحفظ ذلك أم ضيع، حتى يسأل الرجل عن أهل بيته

Indeed Allah (swt) will question everyone who is responsible about his charge, did he preserve it or lost it, until the man will be asked about his family[2].

---

[1] Narrated by: Bukhari (H/5200) and some other places and Muslim (H/1829) narrated from Ibn 'Umar (may Allaah be pleased with them).

[2] Narrated by Tirmidhi after (Hadith Number/1705), al-Nisaa'i in al-Kubra (H/9129), Ibn Hibban in his (book) Sahih Ibn Hibban (h/4492), and graded it as Hasan, from Anas as *Marfu* Hadith', it has been narrated from Qatada from al-Hasan from the Prophet as *Mursal* Hadith, It is *Saheeh* as said by Bukhaari.

2. Call of the Fitrah (nature/instinct), and the demand of the wise men to purify their homes (in sense and meaning) and their aspiration for their homes, and those living inside them, to be the finest, lofty, and distinctive in terms of (minds and bodies). If Allah (swt) has placed the one who doesn't have the sense of the instinct of preserving homes and protecting the children, then the one who possesses the mind would be more worthy and deserving.

3. Homes have remained and will remain forever, with the permission of Allah (swt), the first forts and fenders from the attacks. The foundations of consciousness are formed there, the passions are built, and the tree of good morals are irrigated, and from these homes emerge the scholars and nobles, and in them are raised the leaders and the honourable. This place should be paid attention to, and the work in it (Nurturing and Reforming – *Tarbiyyah* and *Islah*) should be considered a (lifelong project). It deserves every effort, and every exertion towards it should be enjoyed, and all difficulties should be overcome.

4. Muslim homes and family being targeted in the age of globalization, the invasion of satellite television, the information revolution and various means of communication, which call for tightening the belt, deeply fostering steadfastness in the battle of challenge and resisting the reckless Imitation. Departments, institutions, and centres that adopt planning and building strategies have become competitors in the field of *Tarbiyyah* (Nurturing).

Hence, the inevitability of discussing homes - how to defend, raise their level, and protect and treat our homes.

Taking care of homes and paying attention to them is aimed at pushing away frustration and despair and raising the level of work and achievement (as much as we can) in the time of defeat and surrender. It is also aimed at transforming the (act of) complaining and blaming enemies into productive work and raising the level of optimism

إذا قال الرجل هلك الناس فهو أهلكهم

If the man says people perish, then he is the most perished among them[3].

5. With regards to the sense of responsibility about the importance of *Tarbiyyah* (Nurturing) and the protection of homes, we see that there is some bafflement and inattention - among some people- and weakness in *Tarbiyyah* (Nurturing), and involvement with the lowest rather than the highest, resulting in straying and corruption. The guardians are complaining about it. The way to *Islah* (reform) is *Tarbiyyah* (Nurturing), attention, returning positive roles to homes, and correcting the path.

6. To be honest and just, there is some awareness, a sense of responsibility, and the train of *Islah* (reform) is moving, and a sense of honour is growing. These positive emotions and noble values are worth appreciation and respect that

---

[3] Narrated by Muslim (h/2623), from Abu Hurayrah.

contribute to charting the course and shaping the map for *Islah* (reform).

7. The fruits of this awareness and the outputs of Tranquil homes stimulate and encourage paying attention towards homes and nurturing their inhabitants. They are decor, pride, and beauty in this World, and they are a store (of), reward, supplication, righteousness, and a relation in the Hereafter. The Prophet (Peace be upon him) said:

فإذا مات ابن آدم انقطع عمله إلا من ثلاث، وذكر منها (ولد صالح يدعو له)

When a man dies, his acts come to an end, but three, which include (a pious son, who prays for him).[4]

8. At the beginning and at the end, the homes remain our place to rest and comfort, a place where we eat, drink, and marry, the place of our secrets, and our sanctuary in case of good and bad, and the best place in times of discord and scourge. It has been narrated in a *Khabar*,

طوبى لمن ملك لسانه، ووسعه بيته، وبكى على خطيئته

Blessed is the one who controlled his tongue, expanded his home, and wept on his sin.[5]

---

[4] Narrated by Muslim (h/1631), from Abu Hurayrah
[5] Narrated by al-Tabaraani in al-Awsat, h/2340; and al-Sagheer (h/212); graded as Hasan, from Thauban and Abu Na'im in al-Hilyatul Awliya. It is graded as Hasan by Albaani in Saheeh al-Jame' al-Saghir (4/14)

Therefore, our homes deserve our attention as we don't exert many efforts towards their *Tarbiyyah* (Nurturing)

9. There are texts in the Book (Holy Qur'an), Sunnah (sayings and acts of the Prophet (peace be upon him)), and models in the Prophet's biography that talk about homes, indulge on the matter and reveal objectives and effects. There are contemporary and successful experiences in the field of educating homes. Compiling these texts and the experiences together, linking them, and taking guidance from their parameters, is a great thing that deserves our attention, consideration, and authorship.

An Introduction to Homes and its Intricacies

Types of homes and their differentiation (ranking):

It is better to identify the homes mentioned in the Holy Book and Sunnah or the Prophetic Biography, which are many and differ in rank. They include:

1. The homes of Allah.

These are the most honourable and most revered of homes:-

These homes include the one that is located in heaven. Allah (swt) says

$$﴿وَٱلْبَيْتِ ٱلْمَعْمُورِ ٤﴾$$

"And by the ʿSacredʾ Home frequently visited - Baitul Ma'moor"

[TMQ At-Tur – 4]

Ali and Ibn Abbaas (may Allah (swt) be pleased with them) and others said:

هو بيت في السماء حيال الكعبة يدخله كل يوم سبعون ألف ملك ثم يخرجون منه

فلا يعودون إليه

it is a home in the heaven directly above the Ka'ba, every day seventy thousand angels enter it, after they come out, they never return.[6]

It has been narrated in Saheeh Muslim that Baitul Ma'moor was raised to the Prophet (during the night of Isra'), and Jibril informed him

أن هذا البيت يدخله كل يوم سبعون ألف ملك إذا خرجوا منه لم يعودوا إليه

That seventy thousand angels enter it daily, after they come out, they never return.[7]

Some homes are found on the Earth, such as mosques.

﴿فِى بُيُوتٍ أَذِنَ ٱللَّهُ أَن تُرْفَعَ وَيُذْكَرَ فِيهَا ٱسْمُهُۥ يُسَبِّحُ لَهُۥ فِيهَا بِٱلْغُدُوِّ وَٱلْآصَالِ ۝ رِجَالٌ لَّا تُلْهِيهِمْ تِجَٰرَةٌ وَلَا بَيْعٌ عَن ذِكْرِ ٱللَّهِ وَإِقَامِ ٱلصَّلَوٰةِ وَإِيتَآءِ ٱلزَّكَوٰةِ يَخَافُونَ يَوْمًا تَتَقَلَّبُ فِيهِ ٱلْقُلُوبُ وَٱلْأَبْصَٰرُ ۝﴾

"'That light shines' through homes 'of worship' which Allah (swt) has ordered to be raised, and where His Name is mentioned. He is glorified there morning and evening} {People...}"

[TMQ An-Nur – 36-37]

The most revered among these mosques is Masjid Al-haram

﴿إِنَّ أَوَّلَ بَيْتٍ وُضِعَ لِلنَّاسِ لَلَّذِى بِبَكَّةَ مُبَارَكًا وَهُدَى لِّلْعَلَمِينَ ٩٦﴾

"Surely the first Home ʿof worshipʾ established for humanity is the one at Bakkah—a blessed sanctuary and a guide for ʿallʾ people"

[TMQ Ali 'Imran – 96]

Praying in it is equal to praying one thousand prayers at other places; this has been established by the prophet (peace be upon him)[8].

How lucky and blessed is the one who frequently prayed in this Masjid. It is followed by the Mosque of Prophet (Peace be upon him) in Medinah. Praying in it is equal to one thousand prayers at other places[9], and lucky is the one who is keen on praying in there. These two mosques are followed by Al-Aqsa mosque (may Allah (swt) bless it with freedom), where offering prayers one time is equal to praying five hundred times[10].

May Allah (swt) provide us with (the opportunity) to pray in it before we die and set it free from the hands of the tyrants. Then the most honorable homes on earth are the mosques (except the three mentioned above) found on earth, as they are the places for worship, knowledge, and learning. The one whose thoughts remain stuck with the mosque is one among the seven who will be

---

[8] Bukhari (h/1190) and Muslim (h/1394) narrated from Abu Hurayrah (may Allah be pleased with him)

[9] The previous hadith. It is authenticated by both Bukhari and Muslim

[10] Narrated by Bazzar in al-Musnad (h/4142) from Abu Darda'. He described its chain of narration as Hasan

blessed with the shade of the Almighty Allah (swt) on the Day when there will be no shade but His.[11]

2. Homes of Previous Prophets (Peace be upon them)

We see Noah seeking forgiveness for himself, his parents, whoever entered his home in faith, and for believers both male and female

﴿رَّبِّ ٱغْفِرْ لِي وَلِوَٰلِدَيَّ وَلِمَن دَخَلَ بَيْتِيَ مُؤْمِنًا وَلِلْمُؤْمِنِينَ وَٱلْمُؤْمِنَٰتِ وَلَا تَزِدِ ٱلظَّٰلِمِينَ إِلَّا تَبَارًا ۝٢٨﴾

"My Lord! Forgive me, my parents, and whoever enters my home in faith, and ˹all˺ believing men and women"   [TMQ Nuh – 28]

We also see Ibrahim (peace be upon him) praying when he settled his family in a barren valley (by command of Allah), he says

﴿رَّبَّنَآ إِنِّي أَسْكَنتُ مِن ذُرِّيَّتِي بِوَادٍ غَيْرِ ذِى زَرْعٍ عِندَ بَيْتِكَ ٱلْمُحَرَّمِ رَبَّنَا لِيُقِيمُواْ ٱلصَّلَوٰةَ فَٱجْعَلْ أَفْـِٔدَةً مِّنَ ٱلنَّاسِ تَهْوِىٓ إِلَيْهِمْ وَٱرْزُقْهُم مِّنَ ٱلثَّمَرَٰتِ لَعَلَّهُمْ يَشْكُرُونَ ۝٣٧﴾

"Our Lord! I have settled some of my offspring in a barren valley, near Your Sacred Home, our Lord, so that they may establish prayer. So make the hearts of ˹believing˺ people incline towards them and provide them with fruits, so perhaps they will be thankful"   [TMQ Ibrahim – 37]

---

[11] Narrated by Bukhari (h/660) and at some other places, Muslim (h/1031) by Abu Hurayrah

Musa and Haroon, peace be upon them, when they were restricted in their worship by the tyrants, being revealed

﴿وَأَوْحَيْنَآ إِلَىٰ مُوسَىٰ وَأَخِيهِ أَن تَبَوَّءَا لِقَوْمِكُمَا بِمِصْرَ بُيُوتًا وَٱجْعَلُوا۟ بُيُوتَكُمْ قِبْلَةً وَأَقِيمُوا۟ ٱلصَّلَوٰةَ وَبَشِّرِ ٱلْمُؤْمِنِينَ ۝﴾

"We revealed to Moses and his brother, "Appoint homes for your people in Egypt. Turn these homes into places of worship"   [TMQ Yunus – 87]

It means: turn your places of residence into mosques where you will offer prayers.[12]

3. Homes of Prophet Mohammed (Peace be upon him)

These are the rooms of his wives, the mothers to all believers (may Allah (swt) be pleased with them). These are the places where the *Ayaat* of Allah (swt) and Wisdom were recited. These houses are the most purified and most sacred among the homes of the Muslim Ummah and have their special etiquettes and rulings.

4. Homes of those who lived during the best of the times, the companions of the Prophet Peace be upon him (may Allah (swt) be pleased with them).

---

[12] Tafsir al-Qurtubi (6/595)

These are the homes of *Iman* (belief), knowledge, call (towards Islam), and *Ihsan* (benevolence). It may be sufficient to refer to two examples. In Mecca, Dar al-Arqam[13] (the home of Arqam bin Abi'l Arqam, may Allah (swt) be pleased with him), which served as the first station of the *Da'wah* (towards Islam) and the place where believers held their meetings. In Medina, the home of Abu Ayub al-Ansari (may Allah (swt) be pleased with him) where the Prophet (peace be upon him) lived when he (peace be upon him) first arrived in Medina.[14] Overall, the homes of the companions (*Sahaba*) at any place are examples of purity, *Iman* (belief), and chastity. We will discuss some of these homes in the coming pages.

5. Homes of Muslims generally

through the sequence of time and the difference of place. These are what we intend to discuss here.

6. Homes of those that don't possess any sense:

There are homes of some creatures of Allah (swt) that don't possess any sense. However, they are mentioned in the Holy Qur'an for wisdom and purpose. The (Spider) built a home, even though it is the weakest home

---

[13] Tabaqat al-Kubra by Ibn S'ad (3/242)
[14] Narrated by Bukhari (h/3911) and Muslim (h/524) from Anas (may Allah be pleased with him).

﴿مَثَلُ ٱلَّذِينَ ٱتَّخَذُواْ مِن دُونِ ٱللَّهِ أَوْلِيَآءَ كَمَثَلِ ٱلْعَنكَبُوتِ ٱتَّخَذَتْ بَيْتًا وَإِنَّ أَوْهَنَ ٱلْبُيُوتِ لَبَيْتُ ٱلْعَنكَبُوتِ لَوْ كَانُواْ يَعْلَمُونَ ۝﴾

"And the flimsiest of all shelters is certainly that of a spider"

[TMQ Al-Ankabut – 41]

Allah (swt) made this parable in the home of the spider for those (polytheists) who take gods other than Him. These gods do not benefit them or harm them, such as the spider's shelter that does not protect it from heat and cold.[15]

The homes of (bees) have been mentioned as a lesson. They are more cohesive, and there is no imbalance in their home. The bees, even if they roamed in the mountains and trees and flew in the vast wildlands and the deep valleys, they return to their homes without loosing way of their homes. They build the wax from their wings, preserve the honey from those inside, hatch the nestlings from their backs,[16] and in that is a sign and a lesson.

Therefore, if the Holy Qur'an pays attention to the homes of those who have no sense, then those who possess intellect should pay attention to their homes, and deal in the best manner with the dwellers of these homes, and undertake their *Tarbiyyah* (Nurturing) and *Islah* (Reform).

---

[15] Al-Jami' li Ahkam al-Qru'an by Qurtubi)(13/349)
[16] Tafsir Ibn Kathir (2/937)

Homes (mentioned) in the Holy Qur'an

There are many purposes and benefits of homes (mentioned) in the *ayaat* of the Holy Qur'an. There are subtleties and secrets of homes worthy of contemplation and reflection, this includes:

1. Homes are a Blessing

Allah (swt) says at the beginning of his discussion about His (swt) favors

$$\text{﴿وَٱللَّهُ جَعَلَ لَكُم مِّنْ بُيُوتِكُمْ سَكَنًا ..﴾}$$

"Allah (swt) has made your homes a place of rest for you"

[TMQ An Nahl – 80]

This means that Allah's ultimate favor and blessing upon his servants is that he made them these homes where they find shelter, a place to cover and achieve all kinds of benefits.[17]

There is no doubt that those who have lost the blessing of the homes, such as displaced and refugees, understand it perhaps more than others. May Allah (swt) provide shelter for every displaced Muslim.

2. Homes are a place to store and a repository of secrets:

---

[17] Tafsir Ibn Kathir (4/509)

Allah (swt) says:

$$\text{﴾... وَأُنَبِّئُكُم بِمَا تَأْكُلُونَ وَمَا تَدَّخِرُونَ فِي بُيُوتِكُمْ ...﴿٤٩﴾}$$

"And I will prophesize what you eat and store in your homes"

[TMQ Ali' Imran – 49]

Even if the verse was revealed in the context of the miracles of Isa (peace be upon him), the verse uncovers the task of (storing) foods in homes, of which some is eaten on the same day, and some is stored for the following day or the day after.[18] Homes, with their walls and roofs, are the repository of the secrets of its residents. The knowledge about the food, whether less or more, sufficient or insufficient to fulfil the need, can't be known. This is a secret and cover (provided by) Allah (swt) for the residents of the homes so that the gloaters do not rejoice over them. We thank Allah (swt) for making our homes a cover for us.

3. Homes are (turned into) places of worship

When Muslims are restricted from praying in mosques, they are commanded to turn their homes into places of worship

$$\text{﴾وَأَوْحَيْنَا إِلَىٰ مُوسَىٰ وَأَخِيهِ أَن تَبَوَّءَا لِقَوْمِكُمَا بِمِصْرَ بُيُوتًا وَاجْعَلُوا بُيُوتَكُمْ}$$
$$\text{قِبْلَةً وَأَقِيمُوا الصَّلَاةَ ۗ وَبَشِّرِ الْمُؤْمِنِينَ ﴿٨٧﴾﴿}$$

---

[18] Tafsir Qurtubi (4/95)

"We revealed to Moses and his brother, "Appoint homes for your people in Egypt. Turn these homes into places of worship, establish prayer'

[TMQ Yunus – 87]

It has been explained earlier.

4. Homes are places of deterrence and reducing the opportunities of corruption:

Don't you see that Allah (swt) says:

﴿وَٱلَّٰتِى يَأْتِينَ ٱلْفَٰحِشَةَ مِن نِّسَآئِكُمْ فَٱسْتَشْهِدُواْ عَلَيْهِنَّ أَرْبَعَةً مِّنكُمْ فَإِن شَهِدُواْ فَأَمْسِكُوهُنَّ فِى ٱلْبُيُوتِ حَتَّىٰ يَتَوَفَّىٰهُنَّ ٱلْمَوْتُ أَوْ يَجْعَلَ ٱللَّهُ لَهُنَّ سَبِيلًا ۝﴾

""As for" those of your women who commit illegal intercourse—call four witnesses from among yourselves. If they testify, confine the offenders to their homes until they die or Allah (swt) ordains a "different" way for them"
[TMQ An Nisa' – 15]

Qurtubi said: This is the first punishment against adultery, which happened in the early period of Islam and was nullified later.[19] Ibn Kathir noted it was annulled by lashing or stoning in Surah An-Nur, which is an established matter in Ummah.[20]

---

[19] Aljami' li Ahkam al-Quran (5/84)
[20] Tafsir Ibn Kathir (2/204)

5. Home is the place for (spending the mandatory period of) *Iddah* for the divorced woman:

Allah (swt) says:

$$\text{﴿يَٰٓأَيُّهَا ٱلنَّبِيُّ إِذَا طَلَّقْتُمُ ٱلنِّسَآءَ فَطَلِّقُوهُنَّ لِعِدَّتِهِنَّ وَأَحْصُوا۟ ٱلْعِدَّةَ وَٱتَّقُوا۟ ٱللَّهَ رَبَّكُمْ لَا تُخْرِجُوهُنَّ مِنْ بُيُوتِهِنَّ ..﴾}$$

"O Prophet! 'Instruct the believers:' When you 'intend to' divorce women, then divorce them with concern for their waiting period, and count it accurately. And fear Allah, your Lord. Do not force them out of their homes, nor should they leave"　　　　　　　[TMQ At-Talaq: 1]

The wisdom behind this ruling is that it significantly protects modesty. The divorcee woman becomes the sight of attention, and rumors could spread, causing a great dispute (in opinions), and hardly any just person would ever defend her. Therefore, the housing was legislated in her favor.[21]

6. Homes are for setting examples and (drawing) lessons.

The homes of the spider and the bee have been mentioned earlier.

---

[21] Ibn Ashur: At Tahrir wat Tanvir (28/304). Refer to: Al-Buyut fil Kitab was Sunnah: Zaid (p 261), it carries more detail.

Homes That Had A (Distinct) Place And Effect During The Period Of Prophet (peace be upon him)

It is challenging to account for all Muslim homes that impacted the course of history. I will point out some homes during the period of Prophet (peace be upon him) and their significance and lessons.

1. **The Home of al-Arqam bin Al-Arqam (May Allah (swt) be pleased with him);**

The station from which the call (for Islam) started in the most challenging conditions:

It was located on top of Mount Safa and was owned by al-Arqam. Although being young at that time, he was among the early few people who embraced Islam.[22] This home achieved its fame for being the shelter of Muslims during the secrecy phase in Mecca and the place from which Islam was propagated. Believers held meetings there, learned (Islam), and had discussions among themselves. Many people embraced Islam there. When Omar (may Allah (swt) be pleased with him) entered Islam, the believers came out of this home, chanted (AllahuAkbar), and circumambulated the Ka'ba openly.[23]

---

[22] Al-Zahbi: As Siyar (2/479)
[23] Ibn S'ad: Tabqat (3/422 – 243)

2. **The Home of Abu Bakr Al-Siddiq (May Allah (swt) be pleased with him)**

And the event of the Major Migration:

The journey of major migration started from this home, which changed the course of history. It was this home where the migration from Mecca to Medina was planned and prepared. Bukhari and others have narrated from Aisha (may Allah (swt) be pleased with her), she said:

بينما نحن جلوس في بيت أبي بكر في نحر الظهيرة، قال قائل لأبي بكر: هذا رسول الله متقنعًا في ساعة لم يكن يأتينا فيها، فقال أبوبكر: فدى له أبي وأمي، والله ما جاء به في هذه الساعة إلا أمر

One day, while we were sitting in Abu Bakr's home at noon, someone said to Abu Bakr, "This is Allah's Messenger (Peace be upon him) with his head covered, coming at a time at which he never used to visit us before." Abu Bakr said, "May my parents be sacrificed for him. By Allah, he has not come at this hour except for a great necessity. [24]

The Prophet (peace be upon him) and Abu Bakr (may Allah (swt) be pleased with him) started planning and preparing for the migration. What is to be considered here is the fact that the home of Abu Bakr (may Allah (swt) be pleased with him) and his family assisted in the event of migration (young and old, male and female, and their slaves). One made preparations (Asma bint Abu Bakr may Allah (swt) be pleased with her), other spent nights with them (i.e

---

[24] Sahih Bukhari (h/3905), Musnad Ahmad (6/346), Tabqat Ibn Sa'd (8/250)

the Meccan Polytheists) and gathered information (Abdullah bin Abu Bakr, may Allah (swt) be pleased with him), and another grazed his sheep in order to remove the footprints and provide them (i.e the two migrants) with milk (Amir bin Fuhaira, the slave of Abu Bakr, may Allah (swt) be pleased with him). [25]

This way, the honorable household served the Prophet (peace be upon him) and managed the journey of the major migration. What an honorable home and what a beautiful *Tarbiyyah* (Nurturing) with which Abu Bakr raised his family and his slaves (may Allah (swt) be pleased with them all). The homes of believers should be like that.

3. **Home of Abu Ayyub al-Ansari, may Allah (swt) be pleased with him,**

The first residence of the Prophet (peace be upon him) in Medina:

This home was in Medina. It had the honor of embracing and sheltering Prophet Mohammad (peace be upon him) when he first arrived in Medina. The arrival of the Prophet (peace be upon him) in the courtyard of Abu Ayyub Ansari has been validated in Bukhari and Muslim.[26]

Abu Ayyub (Khalid bin Zaid, may Allah (swt) be pleased with him) had the honor over others to take the camel of the Prophet (peace

---

[25] For more, refer to, Al-Mukhtasar min Sahih Al-Sirah by Dr. Sulaiman Al-Odah (P 166)

[26] Bukhari (h/3911), Muslim (h/524) narrated from Anas bin Malik, may Allah be pleased with him.

be upon him) and bring her into his home. The Prophet (peace be upon him) said,

$$\text{المرء مع رحله}$$

"the man is with his conveyance."

The prophet (Peace be upon him) resided there for seven months[27]. You can imagine the blessings landing in this home where the guest is the Prophet (Peace be upon him), and the host is one of the most eminent persons among the Ansaar (the companions of Prophet peace be upon him in Medina).

4. **The Home of Anas bin Malik, may Allah (swt) be pleased with him,**

The conductor of brotherhood among the Muhajiroon (i.e the migrants) and the Ansaar (i.e the helpers)

He was the servant of the Prophet (Peace be upon him). His mother raised him in her home and she gave him good *Tarbiyyah* (Nurturing) until she left him with the Prophet (Peace be upon him) to serve him.[28] He moved from an honourable home (a model for *Tarbiyyah* (Nurturing)) into the home of Prophethood (the most honourable home). This shows us the role of the woman in raising and undertaking the *Tarbiyyah* (Nurturing) of the young.

The home of Anas (may Allah (swt) be pleased with him), later, had the honour of establishing brotherhood among the Muhajiroon (i.e

---

[27] Tabqat Ibn Sa'd (1/237)
[28] Sahih Muslim (h/2481)

the migrants) and Ansar (i.e the helpers). Bukhari and Muslim narrate from Anas (may Allah (swt) be pleased with him): Prophet (Peace be upon him) made a treaty (of brotherhood) between the Quraish and the Ansar in my home[29].

Ibn Saad reports that the Prophet made a treaty (of brotherhood) between Quraish and Ansar in the home of Anas (may Allah (swt) be pleased with him)[30]. You can imagine the greatness of this task – establishing brotherhood – emerging from the home of Anas bin Malik (may Allah (swt) be pleased with him), what a blessed treaty and what a blessed home.

The discussion will stretch if we keep reflecting upon the impact of the homes of the *Sahaba* (the companions of the Prophet Peace be upon him). We will stick to exploring their effects as these homes left us great and noble personalities in knowledge, Da'wah (calling towards Islam), and Jihad, like Abdullah bin Abbas, Abdullah bin Omar, and Abdullah bin Zubayr (may Allah (swt) be pleased with them all), and there are many like them. This establishes that each home of the *Sahaba* possessed an incubator for *Tarbiyyah* (i.e Nurturing).[31]

5. Home of Ramla bint Harith al-Ansariyah an-Najariyah and her husband Ma'az bin Harith bin Rufa'h, may Allah (swt) be pleased with them.

---

[29] Bukhari (h/6083) and some other places, Muslim (h/2052)
[30] Tabqat (1/239)
[31] Duatun fil Buyut by Dr. Salman Al-Odah (P 13-14)

The People of Banu Qurayza were imprisoned in her home when Sa'd bin Ma'az rendered the decree concerning them.[32]

Books containing biographies have mentioned some other roles of the home of Ramla (may Allah (swt) be pleased with her). The various delegations who visited Prophet (Peace be upon him) used to stay there. Her home witnessed a treaty being written between the Prophet (Peace be upon him) and the Jews. The furniture, belongings, and clothes of Banu Qurayza were also deposited there. Safana, the sister of Adi bin Hatim (may Allah (swt) be pleased with her), also stayed there in addition to other roles and tasks of this home. [33]

Thus, the contemplating party realizes the abundance and comprehensiveness of the homes of *Sahaba* in serving (Islam) during the periods of Mecca and Medina, by both high ranking and low ranking *Sahaba*, men and women, which points to the fact that the homes of *Sahaba* played various roles in the service of Islam and raising those who dwelled in these homes, and their active participation in life.

---

[32] Al-Isabah by Ibj Hajar (12/259-260)
[33] For more, please refer to the Al-Mukhtasar min Sahih As Sirah (P. 386)

Islam's Early Devotion Towards Homes

1. Selection of the spouses

The Husband and wife are the pillars of a home. Those who built their homes on (the principle of) fearing Allah, the almighty, and (seeking) His pleasure are not similar to those who founded it on the edge of a crumbling cliff. While the success comes from Allah, however, it is necessary to create the causes for *Islah* (i.e, reform) of homes by choosing the spouses. Prophet Peace be upon him said:

فاظفر بذات الدين تربت يداك

"get the one who is religious and prosper".

The hadith has been authenticated by Bukhari and Muslim.

The world is a temporary comfort, and the best temporary comfort of this world is a righteous woman.[34] The woman is the primary pillar of the home, an essential element in the *Tarbiyyah* (i.e, Nurturing), and more caring towards home. She is perhaps closer to the children; therefore, her contribution in upbringing (the children) is vital. Choosing her or educating her about the rightness and reformation is a necessity. Attaining a righteous woman is a blessing of Allah (swt) for the man. Allah, the almighty, mentioned His favour on the prophet Zakariyyah (peace be upon him) with Islaah of his wife

---

[34] Muslim (h/1467) narrated from Abdullah bin Umar (may Allah be pleased with them).

﴿.. وَأَصْلَحْنَا لَهُۥ زَوْجَهُۥٓ ..۝﴾

"and made his wife fertile"   [TMQ Al-Anbiya – 90]

In contrast, He also mentioned the punishment of betrayal by wife, such as in the example of the wives of Noah and Lot

﴿.. فَخَانَتَاهُمَا فَلَمْ يُغْنِيَا عَنْهُمَا مِنَ ٱللَّهِ شَيْـًٔا وَقِيلَ ٱدْخُلَا ٱلنَّارَ مَعَ ٱلدَّٰخِلِينَ۝﴾

"So their husbands were of no benefit to them against Allah (swt) whatsoever. Both were told, "Enter the Fire, along with the others!"
[TMQ At-Tahrim: 10]

The husband is the custodian of the home, the owner of the moral strength and religious (values), and appointed, with the permission of Allah, to reform (i.e undertake *Islah*) at his home. Hence, the focus has been put on the (proposing) man who possess moral strength and is religious

إذا أتاكم من ترضون دينه وخُلقه فزوجوه، إلا تفعلوا تكن فتنة في الأرض وفساد عريض

(If there comes to you one with whose character and religious commitment you are pleased, then marry (your daughter or female relative under your care) to him, for if you do not do that there will be Fitnah in the land and widespread corruption.)[35]

---

[35] Narrated by Ibn Maja (h/1967), Tirmidhi (h/1084), Albani graded it as "hasan" in Sahih Al-Jami al-Saghir (1/134).

The home that establishes its principles on the righteous husband and wife is worthy of becoming successful by itself and producing a generation that Allah, the almighty will use for the benefit of the land and the people.

The door for repentance is open. There are many homes whose fabric got straightened by returning and reforming the spouses after wandering and being lost. They became the best of the homes

$$\text{﴿وَٱلْبَلَدُ ٱلطَّيِّبُ يَخْرُجُ نَبَاتُهُۥ بِإِذْنِ رَبِّهِۦ ۖ وَٱلَّذِى خَبُثَ لَا يَخْرُجُ إِلَّا نَكِدًا ۚ ٥٨ ..﴾}$$

"The fertile land produces abundantly by the Will of its Lord, whereas the infertile land hardly produces anything"   [TMQ Al-A'raf – 58]

2. Saying the prayer when entering and arriving home:

In addition to choosing spouses, we should seek Tawfeeq and righteousness from Allah (swt) for our homes. Supplication is the easiest and most important way in seeking *Islah* (reform) in homes. We must ask Allah (swt) and move towards Him with truth and sincerity to achieve *Islah* (reform) in our homes and protect them from the *Shayateen* (from the humans and Djinns). The Holy Qur'an guided the Prophet Noah (peace be upon him)

$$\text{﴿وَقُل رَّبِّ أَنزِلْنِى مُنزَلًا مُّبَارَكًا وَأَنتَ خَيْرُ ٱلْمُنزِلِينَ ٢٩﴾}$$

"And pray, "My Lord! Allow me a blessed landing, for You are the best accommodator"   [TMQ Al-Mu'minun – 29]

Qurtubi said: "the verse is a teaching from Allah (swt) to His servants so that they say it when they board a travel vehicle and when they arrive, and even when they enter their homes and offer greetings. [36]

The Prophet (Peace be upon him) guided us to be supported by the effect of the supplication when arriving at a destination. He (Peace be upon him) said:

من نزل منزلًا فقال: أعوذ بكلمات الله التامات من شر ما خلق، لم يضره شيء

حتى يرتحل من منزله ذلك

Whosoever alights somewhere and says, "I seek refuge in the Perfect Words of Allah (swt) from the evil of what He has created," nothing will harm him until he departs from that place."[37]

So you see, what a lucky person is he, who doesn't miss this prayer when arriving somewhere and its effect, is, as we learned?

3. Supplication when copulating:

As much Islam is interested in fortifying homes when entering them by *Dhikr* (remembrance) and *Du'aa* (Supplication)', it also pays attention to when building the first blocks of the home – The offspring. It guides to another *Du'aa* when having intercourse. It explains its effect on the newborn, and in that, the Prophet (Peace be upon him) says:

---

[36] Aljami li Ahkam al-Quran (12/120)
[37] Muslim (h/2708)

لو أن أحدكم إذا أراد أن يأتي أهله قال: بسم الله، اللهم جنبنا الشيطان وجنب الشيطان ما رزقتنا، فإنه إن قضى بينهما ولد من ذلك لم يضره الشيطان أبدًا

(if anyone who means to have intercourse with his wife says, "In the name of God. O God, keep us away from the devil and keep the devil away from what Thou hast provided us," should it be ordained that a child be born to them thereby, no devil will ever harm it.)[38]

Is this not early attention and care? Can this Du'aa be left, which is a way to protect the baby from the cursed Shaytaan? The Prophet (Peace be upon him) also advised this prayer to a *Sahabi* couple when they lost their son so that the replacement (new baby) is noble.

4. Choosing a spacious home and righteous neighbor

Islam guides us to choose a spacious home where hearts are delighted, happiness befalls, and (the residents) thank the knower of the unseen. Hence, the Prophet Peace be upon him said:

أربع من السعادة: المرأة الصالحة، والمسكن الواسع، والجار الصالح، والمركب الهني

(Four things are (the sign of) bliss: righteous woman, spacious residence, righteous neighbor, easy conveyance...)[39]

---

[38] Bukhari (h/6388) Muslim (h/1434)
[39] Ibn Habban (h/4032), Hilyat al-Awliya (8/388) from Sa'd bin Abi Waqqas (may Allah be pleased with him), Musnad Ahmad (h/1445), Mustadrak al-Hakim (h/2640). Albani graded it "Sahih": Sahih al-Jami' (1/305).

The righteous neighbor helps his neighbor in doing the right acts and staying away from disliked and prohibited matters. The reality is evident in the impact of the neighbor. Many neighbors have become the reason for the happiness and righteousness of their neighbors. If they saw good, they became happy and encouraged their neighbor, and if they saw otherwise, they concealed it and gave advice. Therefore, it is said (Choose your neighbor before your home).

The proximity with the mosque while choosing the home also helps. The mosque is the place where the *Dhikr* of Allah (swt) is established, and the family listens to the call of the Prayer (*Aadhan*), the recitation of the Qur'an, and *Dhikr*. All these things help the family in obeying Allah, reforming homes, establishing prayers, urges the children to join the Qur'an memorization sessions.

Therefore, we should select the places of our homes, inquire about the neighborhood, be good with neighbors, and increase in our expression of thanks to Almighty Allah, as our homes are a blessing and favor from our Lord.

5. **Preserving the dignity of homes and the etiquette of seeking permission (to enter)**

Homes have secrets as well as dignities that must be preserved and maintained. Allah (swt) made seeking permission a tool to protect these secrets and dignities. He made it obligatory for Muslims to seek permission, as He said

$$\langle\!\langle \text{يَـٰٓأَيُّهَا ٱلَّذِينَ ءَامَنُوا۟ لَا تَدْخُلُوا۟ بُيُوتًا غَيْرَ بُيُوتِكُمْ حَتَّىٰ تَسْتَأْنِسُوا۟ وَتُسَلِّمُوا۟ عَلَىٰٓ} $$

$$\text{أَهْلِهَا ۚ ذَٰلِكُمْ خَيْرٌ لَّكُمْ لَعَلَّكُمْ تَذَكَّرُونَ ۝ فَإِن لَّمْ تَجِدُوا۟ فِيهَآ أَحَدًا فَلَا}$$

$$\text{تَدْخُلُوهَا حَتَّىٰ يُؤْذَنَ لَكُمْ ۖ وَإِن قِيلَ لَكُمُ ٱرْجِعُوا۟ فَٱرْجِعُوا۟ ۖ هُوَ أَزْكَىٰ لَكُمْ ۚ وَٱللَّهُ}$$

$$\text{بِمَا تَعْمَلُونَ عَلِيمٌ ۝} \rangle\!\rangle$$

"O, believers! Do not enter any home other than your own until you have asked for permission and greeted its occupants. This is best for you, so perhaps you will be mindful} {If you find no one at home, do not enter it until you have been given permission. And if you are asked to leave, then leave. That is purer for you. And Allah (swt) has ʿperfectʾ knowledge of what you do" [TMQ An-Nur 27 – 28]

Ibn Kathir, may Allah (swt) have mercy upon him, said: these are *Shari'* etiquettes taught by Allah (swt) to His servants in seeking permission. He commanded them not to enter any homes other than theirs until they seek approval before entry and offer greetings after being allowed to enter.[40]

Seeking permission allows homes their sanctity and saves the residents from the disturbance caused by sudden entry, the annoyance by the unexpected (access), and getting hurt from the exposure of *Awrah* (Parts of the body that are not supposed to be exposed to others.) Perhaps these things were practiced in the pre-Islamic era, and Islam annulled this disturbance and taught Muslims the etiquette of seeking permission.

Asking permission is permissible three times, as has been mentioned in the Sahih Hadith

---

[40] Tafsir Ibn Kathir (3/460) Published by Ehya at Turas Publishing house

إذا استأذن أحدكم ثلاثًا فلم يؤذن له فليرجع

When one of you asks permission three times and if it is not granted to him, he should go away.[41]

When seeking permission to enter, the one asking permission should not face the door but should face towards left or right so that he does not see inside the home.[42]

When Prophet (Peace be upon him) visited someone's home, he would not face (the door) directly, rather towards the right or left pillar.[43]

Prophet (Peace be upon him) also guided us to seek permission when entering (into the private places) of *Maharim* (family members with whom marriage would be considered illegal), such as the mother. Imam Malik narrates from Ata' that the Prophet Peace be upon him was asked by a man saying,

يا رسول الله! أستأذن على أمي؟ قال :نعم، قال الرجل :إني معها في البيت، فقال

رسول الله :استأذن عليها، أتحب أن تراها عُريانة؟ قال :لا، قال فاستأذن عليها

"O Prophet of Allah, should I seek permission to enter from my mother? The Prophet replied, "yes." The man said, "I share the home with her." Prophet Peace be upon him said, "seek her

---

[41] Bukhari (h/6245), Muslim (h/2153)
[42] Al-Jami li Ahkam al-Quran by Qurtubi (12/144), Tafsir Ibn Kathir (3/461)
[43] Narrated by Bukhari in Adab al-Mufrad (h/1078) from hadith of Abudllah bin Basar, may Allah be pleased with him. Albani said when commenting on Al-Adab al-Mufrad it is "Hasan Sahih"

permission; would you like to see her naked? The man said, "No," the Prophet Peace be upon him said, "then ask her permission."[44]

The matter of asking permission is so big that (the violators have been warned with) piercing the eye. A man peeped through a round hole into the dwelling place of the Prophet, while the Prophet (Peace be upon him) had a *Midray* (an iron comb) with which he was scratching his head. the Prophet (Peace be upon him) said,

لو أعلم أنك تنظر لطعنت به عينك، إنما جُعل الاستئذان من أجل البصر

" Had I known you were looking (through the hole), I would have pierced your eye with it (i.e., the comb)." Verily! The order of taking permission to enter has been enjoined because of that sight (that one should not look unlawfully at the state of others). [45]

Since the viewer has demolished the dignity of homes and allowed his eyesight to infiltrate the *Awrah* of others, he thus wasted his eye (if pierced). Therefore, the *Awrah* of Muslims are preserved, and what could maintain the dignity of their homes is prescribed and legislated.

6. Prohibition of things that stop angels from entering home:

Besides the interest (of Islam) in preserving the homes and founding them on (the principles of) righteousness and *Taqwa*

---

[44] Mua'tta (2/963). Abu Amr said "Mursal Sahih
Ibn Hajar authenticated its chain of narration (Al-Fathul Bari – 11/25). Refer to: Ahkam wa Aadab Dukhool al-Bait by Dr. Abdul Karim Khidar Page 20. The researcher favors that seeking permission to entry from *Maharim* is *Wajib*.
[45] Bukhari (h/6241) Muslim (2156)

(fearing Allah), there is something that needs to be taken care of in order to avoid risks and protect the homes. It is a warning to free and save the homes from things that may turn them into a hotbed for *Shayateen* and prevent the close (to Allah) angels from entering them. No Muslim would like to see angels not entering his home, nor would any Muslim like his home to become a hotbed for *Shaytaan*? Therefore, we must consider this guidance, make sense of it, and save ourselves from indulging in it. Ahmad, Tirmidhi, and Ibn Hibban, may Allah (swt) have mercy on them, narrate that Prophet Peace be upon him said

إن الملائكة لا تدخل بيتًا فيه تماثيل أو صور

Angels do not enter the home where there are portrayals or pictures.[46]

In another hadith, the Prophet Peace be upon him said

إن الملائكة لا تدخل بيتًا فيه كلب

Verily, Angels do not enter a home where there is a dog, [47]

and a third hadith says

إن الملائكة لا تدخل بيتًا فيه كلب ولا صورة

Verily, angels do not make entry into a home containing a dog or a portrait.[48]

---

[46] Sahih Al-Jami' al-Saghir (2/167)
[47] The reference mentioned above
[48] The reference mentioned above

There is a consensus (among scholars of Islam) on the prohibition of bringing prohibited portrayals, portraits, and dogs (inside a home). Imam Bukhari named a chapter (Chapter: Angels do not enter a house in which there are pictures), in which he mentioned the hadith and the saying of the Gabriel (peace be upon him)

كلب ولا صورة فيه بيتًا ندخل لا إنا

"We do not enter into a home in which there is a picture or a dog."[49]

In any case, the pictures are what caused the wide spreading of crisis, and these are abundant in homes. The Muslims should take precautions and restrain (from bringing these things into homes) as much as possible, especially things that are prohibited. Some exempt children's games from being prohibited. They base this extraction on the hadith of Aisha (may Allah (swt) be pleased with her)

كنت ألعب بالبنات عند النبي

---

[49] Bukhari (h/5960) transmitted from Ibn Umar, may Allah be pleased with them. Ibn Hajar narrated from Qurtubi, he said: "Angels do not enter the house in which there is a picture, because the one who took this picture inside the house acts like disbelievers who take pictures into their houses and honor them and the angels dislike it" Al-Fathul Bari (10/391-392). Ibn Hajar adds in I'zah, saying "this hadith favors the view that the pictures which restrict the angels from entering the place is the one in which it remains on its original structure, put in higher place not lower; if it is put down or its form/structure is changed either by cutting it by half or by cutting its head, then it doesn't restrict them. Al-Fathul Bari (10/392)

"I used to play with dolls when I was with the Prophet Peace be upon him." [50]

Ibn Hajar commented on this Hadith, mentioned the dispute of scholars on it, and collected them between the *Ahadith* of the prohibition against pictures and this hadith. Whoever wishes may review it.[51]

As for dogs that are forbidden in homes, it is a fascination that affects some people, who raise them, adorn them, and care about their cleanliness and eating, and perhaps name them the best names and may have bought them against large sums. Do they know that Gabriel (peace be upon him) refrained from coming to the Prophet with revelation because of a puppy (a small dog) in the home?[52] Do those who have the dogs in their homes know that they lose two *Qirats* from their rewards daily?[53]

It should be noted that the guarding and hunting dogs are exempted from the forbidden dogs. It should also be noted that the angels meant here are the angels of *barakah* and *rahmah* (kindness and favor), not the angels appointed for saving and writing (the deeds of humans). These angels are not restricted by that, as has been mentioned by al-Khattabi and others.[54]

---

[50] Bukhari (h/5960) Muslim (h/2440)
[51] Al-Fathul Bari (10/527)
[52] Bukhari (h/5960) from Abdullah ibn Umar, may Allah be pleased with them
[53] Bukhari (h/5481) and another place, Muslim (h/1574)
[54] Refer to: These houses are in which Angels do not enter (Ibrahim al-Jamal, Page 52)

Factors Affecting The (Process Of) Tarbiyyah (Nurturing) in Homes

There is no doubt that the guidance (towards the right path) and success in *Islah* (reform) comes from Allah (swt) only. We see corruption and deviation in the homes of chosen and righteous people that are beyond human exertion and beyond the *Tarbiyyah* (Nurturing) of educators and guidance of well-wishers.

Could there be any doubt in the keenness of the messengers and prophets, peace be upon them, on reforming their communities in addition to their homes? However, we still find the deviation in the homes of prophets. Allah (swt) has provided us with parables, He said

﴿ضَرَبَ ٱللَّهُ مَثَلًا لِّلَّذِينَ كَفَرُواْ ٱمْرَأَتَ نُوحٍ وَٱمْرَأَتَ لُوطٍ كَانَتَا تَحْتَ عَبْدَيْنِ مِنْ عِبَادِنَا صَلِحَيْنِ فَخَانَتَاهُمَا فَلَمْ يُغْنِيَا عَنْهُمَا مِنَ ٱللَّهِ شَيْئًا وَقِيلَ ٱدْخُلَا ٱلنَّارَ مَعَ ٱلدَّخِلِينَ ۝﴾

"Allah (swt) sets forth an example for the disbelievers: the wife of Noah and the wife of Lot. Each was married to one of Our righteous servants, yet betrayed them. So their husbands were of no benefit to them against Allah (swt) whatsoever. Both were told, "Enter the Fire, along with the others"

[TMQ At-Tahrim – 10]

Despite that, the man is still responsible for informing, advice, propogation, counseling, and the guidance (towards right path), while making it succeed is in the hands of Allah (swt)

$$\text{﴿إِنَّكَ لَا تَهْدِى مَنْ أَحْبَبْتَ وَلَٰكِنَّ ٱللَّهَ يَهْدِى مَن يَشَآءُ وَهُوَ أَعْلَمُ بِٱلْمُهْتَدِينَ ٥٦﴾}$$

"You surely cannot guide whoever you like ˹O Prophet˺, but it is Allah (swt) Who guides whoever He wills"   [TMQ Al-Qasas – 56]

It is enough for a man to put effort as much as he can in the *Tarbiyyah* (Nurturing) and *Islah* (reform) of the homes. The things that could help him include:

1.   **Sensing and bearing the responsibility of caring:**

Allah (swt) has ordered us, in His holy book, to protect ourselves and our family from the hellfire. He said

$$\text{﴿يَٰأَيُّهَا ٱلَّذِينَ ءَامَنُوا۟ قُوٓا۟ أَنفُسَكُمْ وَأَهْلِيكُمْ نَارًا وَقُودُهَا ٱلنَّاسُ وَٱلْحِجَارَةُ ٦﴾..}$$

"O believers! Protect yourselves and your families from a Fire whose fuel is people and stones"   [TMQ At-Tahrim – 6]

Ali, may Allah (swt) be pleased with him, Qatada, and Mujahid say:

قوا أنفسكم بأفعالكم، وقوا أهليكم بوصيتكم

"Protect yourselves by your acts and protect your family by giving advice."

Al-Qurtubi commented, "this is the right and knowledge required by kindness, the man must reform (*Islah*) himself by obeying and reform his family just as the shepherd cares for his herd.[55] Ilkia al-Hirasi said: "this indicates that we must teach our children and family the religion and the Khayr (i.e the Good) and the necessary etiquette, this is what has been meant by the saying of the Lord

﴿وَأْمُرْ أَهْلَكَ بِالصَّلَوٰةِ وَٱصْطَبِرْ عَلَيْهَا ... ۱۳۲﴾

"command your people to pray, and be diligent in ˹observing˺ it"

[TMQ Taha – 132][56]

and like what He said about Ismai'l, peace be upon him

﴿وَكَانَ يَأْمُرُ أَهْلَهُۥ بِالصَّلَوٰةِ وَٱلزَّكَوٰةِ وَكَانَ عِندَ رَبِّهِۦ مَرْضِيًّا ٥٥﴾

"He used to urge his people to pray and give alms-tax. And his Lord was well pleased with him"   [TMQ Maryam – 55]

Prophet (Peace be upon him) guided us to bear the responsibility to care; he said,

---

[55] Aljami' li Ahkam al-Quran (18/194-195)
[56] Ilkiya al-Hirasi: Ahkam al-Quran (4/488)

ألا كلكم راعٍ، وكلكم مسؤول عن رعيته، فالأمير الذي على الناس راعٍ، وهو مسؤول عن رعيته، والرجل راعٍ على أهل بيته، وهو مسؤول عنهم، والمرأة راعية على بيت بعلها وولده، وهي مسؤولة عنهم، والعبد راعٍ على مال سيده وهو مسؤول عنه، ألا فكلكم راعٍ، وكلكم مسؤول عن رعيته

"All of you are guardians and are responsible for your wards. The ruler is a guardian and is responsible for his subjects, the man is a guardian of his family and is responsible for them, the lady is a guardian and is responsible for her husband's home and his offspring; the slave is guardian of the money of his lord and is responsible for that, so all of you are guardians and are responsible for your wards."[57]

The responsibility of parents in care and upbringing is settled in the *Sharia* and the mind, by urging to obey the Lord and ordering good and forbidding evil, patience and endurance along the way and the difficulties of upbringing, and taking into account the psychology and the challenges of the situation and the weakness of human beings, and their tendency toward complacency and laziness, the whispers of *Shaytan*, and other influences.

There is a misconception among some parents who neglect their children and by which they defend themselves they say, "The guidance is in the hands of Allah." This, although true in its totality, however, does not mean being negligent and having the mere dependence (on Allah (swt)), but it is necessary to undertake the obliged *Asbaab* and diligence in *Tarbiyyah* (Nurturing), carrying out the custodianship (role), and fulfilling the duty of care. The

---

[57] Transmitted by Bukhari (h/5200) and at some other places, Musli (h/1829) the words have been taken from him.

educator (parents) will find the effects of upbringing in reforming (*Islah*), sooner or later. Even if nothing is achieved, providing Tarbiyyah (Nurturing) still possesses an excuse in front of Allah (swt), on the one hand, and there is an achievement of remuneration and reward from Allah (swt), on the other hand. The good word is charity, and what is more significant than it will have a greater reward. However, there is one thing that needs to be considered by parents, which is to start making *Islah* of themselves and to set a role model for children in their behavior and actions before their wordings. The parents' righteousness reaches the children and saves them, God willing. Allah (swt) says in the Holy Qur'an

﴿.. وَكَانَ أَبُوهُمَا صَٰلِحًا ..﴾ (٨٢)

"Their father had been a righteous man"   [TMQ Al-Kahf – 82]

Dear, honourable Parent, Allah (swt) will ask you about the responsibility of care (which he put upon you) in your children, so prepare your answer for the question. Ensure the answer is right, and always remember the saying of the Prophet (Peace be upon him)

إن الله سائل كل راعٍ عما استرعاه، أحفظ ذلك أم ضيَّع، حتى يسأل الرجل عن أهل بيته

"Allah (swt) will ask every guardian about the care (towards the wards who were given in their care), did he preserve it or destroy it, until the man will be asked about his family (members). [58]

2. *Dhikr* (remembrance) of Allah (swt) in Homes:

The hearts feel tranquillity with the *Dhikr* (remembrance) of Allah; the devils get chased away, *barakah* (blessing), and *sakinah* (serenity) are achieved. The homes in which the *Dhikr* of Allah (swt) is common are the most beautiful homes. You can imagine the difference between the homes in which Allah (swt) is remembered and those in which He is not. Sahih Muslim transmits from Abu Musa, may Allah (swt) be pleased with him, who narrates from the Prophet Peace be upon him, who said

مثل البيت الذي يُذكر الله فيه والبيت الذي لا يُذكر الله فيه مثل الحي والميت

"The example of the home in which Allah (swt) is remembered and in comparison to the one in which He is not remembered, is that of a living creature compared to the dead one"[59]

Imam Nawawi, may Allah (swt) have mercy on him, said that the hadith encourages praising Lord in the home and that it should not be left without saying the praises of Allah.[60]

How beautiful is it that the young and the old family members listen to the (*Dhikr*) praises of Allah (swt) making echoes in their

---

[58] Transmitted by Ibn Hubban (h/4493) from the hadith of Hasan al-Basri from the Prophet PBUH. It is *"Mursal"* and Albani graded it *"hasan"* in Sahih al-Jami' (1/365).

[59] Bukhari (h/6407), Musim (h/779) the words belong to Musim.

[60] Commentary of Sahih Muslim (6/68)

homes? The *Dhikr* is an expression of the glory of Allah (swt) and the things He (swt) prohibited. Homes that complain of distress, depression, and satanic temptations, (for them) *Dhikr* is a medicine and (tool for) healing, God willing.

We should listen to the effect of *Dhikr* in homes when a man enters his home, and that is something which people might be missing, so they don't do *Dhikr* when entering their homes. The Prophet Peace be upon him says (When a person enters his home and mentions the name of Allah (swt) at the time of entering it, and while eating the food, Satan says[61]:

إذا دخل الرجل بيته فذكر الله عند دخوله وعند طعامه قال الشيطان: لا مبيت لكم ولا عشاء، وإذا دخل فلم يذكر الله عند دخوله قال الشيطان أدركتم المبيت، وإذا لم يذكر الله عند طعامه قال: أدركتم المبيت والعشاء

"You have no place to spend the night and no evening meal; but when he enters without mentioning the name of Allah, the Satan says: You have found a place to spend the night, and when he does not mention the name of Allah (swt) while eating food, he (the Satan) says: You have found a place to spend the night and evening meal"[62]

Imam Nawawi commented:

وفي هذا استحباب ذكر الله تعالى عند دخول البيت وعند الطعام

This hadith shows that it is *Mustahab* (desired) to mention the name of Allah (swt) when entering the house and when having food.[63]

Similar to mentioning the name of Allah (swt) being *Mustahab* when entering the home as it carries protection and safety, it is also *Mustahab* to remember Allah (swt) when departing the home as it brings protection, defense, and safety. The Prophet Peace be upon him says,

بسم الله، توكلت على الله لا حول ولا قوة إلا بالله، قال: يقال حينئذٍ هديت،

وكفيت، ووقيت، فتنحى عنه الشيطان، فيقول له شيطان آخر: كيف لك برجل

قد هُدي وكُفِي ووُقِي

"When a man goes out of his home and says: "In the name of Allah, I trust in Allah; there is no might and no power but in Allah," the following will be said to him at that time: "You are guided, defended and protected." The devils will go far from him, and another devil will say: How can you deal with a man who has been guided, defended, and protected?"[64]

The structure of home coupled with the *Dhikr* of Allah (swt) is a blessing, bliss, and charity.

Can't the parents distribute *Sadaqat* (charity) in their home each day? Saying "*la ilaha Illal lah*" is a *sadaqah*, saying "*Alhamdu Lillah*" is a *sadaqah*, and saying "*Allahu Akbar*" one time is a *sadaqah*...

---

[63] Commentary of Sahih Muslim (13/190-191)
[64] Abu Dawud (h/5095), Tirmidhi (h/3462), Nasai' in al-Kubra (h/9837) from Anas bin Malik, may Allah be pleased with him. Albani graded it "sahih" in Sahih Abu Dawud (3/959)

Parents should make their children memorize the "*Adhkar*" that have great rewards and are easy to recite, such as the saying of the Prophet Peace be upon him

من قال لا إله إلا الله وحده لا شريك له، له الملك وله الحمد وهو على كل شيء قدير في يوم مائة مرة كانت له عدل عشر رقاب- وفي رواية :من ولد إسماعيل – وكُتبت له مائة حسنة، ومحيت عنه مائة سيئة، وكانت له حرزًا من الشيطان يومه ذلك حتى يمسي، ولم يأتِ أحد بأفضل مما جاء به إلا أحد عمل أكثر من ذلك

"If one says one-hundred times in one day: (None has the right to be worshipped but Allah, the Alone Who has no partners, to Him belongs Dominion and to Him belong all the Praises, and He has power over all things (i.e., Omnipotent)), one will get the reward of manumitting ten slaves, - another narration contains: from the progeny of Isma'il - and one-hundred good deeds will be written in his account, and one-hundred bad deeds will be wiped off or erased from his account, and on that day he will be protected from the morning till evening from Satan, and nobody will be superior to him except one who has done more than that which he has done."[65]

It would be excellent if the parents or any one of them went ahead and read a book about (*Dhikr*) and its virtues, with his/her children, and the family members learned the *Adhkar* of eating, drinking, and wearing, the prayers of the morning, evening, sleeping, when entering into and coming out of the toilet, etc., that will be discussed later in this book.

---

[65] Bukhari (h/3292), Muslim (h/2691), and others

The *Dhikr* includes establishing prayers, especially *Nafl* prayer (supererogatory prayer), inside the home and reciting the Holy Qur'an. Given the importance of these two matters, I will dedicate a special chapter to them.

3. Praying (Salah) inside homes and other *Sunan* (acts and sayings of the Prophet Peace be upon him):

Salah is a link between the servant and his Lord. It is an attribute of Prophets and righteous people

﴿وَكَانَ يَأْمُرُ أَهْلَهُۥ بِٱلصَّلَوٰةِ وَٱلزَّكَوٰةِ وَكَانَ عِندَ رَبِّهِۦ مَرْضِيًّا ۝﴾

"He used to urge his people to pray and give alms-tax"

[TMQ Maryam – 55]

It protects from falling into indecency and sinful things

﴿.. إِنَّ ٱلصَّلَوٰةَ تَنْهَىٰ عَنِ ٱلْفَحْشَآءِ وَٱلْمُنكَرِ وَلَذِكْرُ ٱللَّهِ أَكْبَرُ وَٱللَّهُ يَعْلَمُ مَا تَصْنَعُونَ ۝﴾

"Indeed, ˹genuine˺ prayer should deter ˹one˺ from indecency and wickedness"
[TMQ Al-'Ankabut – 45]

Since mosques are adorned with obligatory prayers, homes should be decorated with *Nafl* prayers_so that angels enter and devils get chased, and the family members learn the virtue of the prayer and how to establish it. This is why we have been urged to establish *Nafl* prayers inside homes and because of the good it carries. The Prophet Peace be upon him said

إذا قضى أحدكم الصلاة في مسجده فليجعل لبيته نصيبًا من صلاته، فإن الله

جاعل في بيته من صلاته خيرًا

"When any one of you observes prayer in the mosque, he should reserve a part of his prayer for his home, for Allah (swt) would make the prayer as a means of betterment in his home"[66]

This prophetic guidance about offering *Nafl* prayers in homes is in order to save them from turning into graves. Therefore, the Prophet Peace be upon him said,

اجعلوا من صلاتكم في بيوتكم، ولا تتخذوها قبورًا

"Offer some of your prayers in your homes, and don't make them graves"[67]

We also have practical guidance from the Prophet (Peace be upon him) in addition to the theoretical guidance. Aisha, may Allah (swt) be pleased with her, informed us about the *Nafl* prayer of the Prophet Peace be upon him in his home, she said,

كان يصلي قبل الظهر أربعًا في بيتي، ثم يخرج فيصلي بالناس، ثم يرجع إلى بيتي فيصلي ركعتين، وكان يصلي بالناس المغرب ثم يرجع إلى بيتي فيصلي ركعتين، وكان يصلي بهم العشاء ثم يدخل بيتي فيصلي ركعتين، وكان يصلي من الليل تسع ركعات فيهن الوتر، وكان يصلي ليلًا طويلًا قائمًا، وليلًا طويلًا قاعدًا

---

[66] Muslim narrated from Jabir, may Allah be pleased with him (h/778).
[67] Transmitted by Bukhari (h/1187) and Muslim (h/777) from Ibn Umar, may Allah be pleased with them.

he used to pray four *raka'hs* in my home before noon, then would go out and lead the people in prayer; then would come into my home and pray two *raka'hs*, then he would lead people in prayer in sunset and return, and pray two *raka'hs*. He would lead the people in prayer at Isha' time, then would enter into my home and pray two *raka'hs*. He used to pray nine *raka'hs*, including "witr" at night, and he would pray while standing for a long time and while sitting for a long time during night..."[68]

The reason behind the urge to pray at home is the great reward for praying *Nafl* (voluntary) prayers in there. Bukhari and Muslim narrate that Prophet Peace be upon him said

فعليكم بالصلاة في بيوتكم، فإن خير صلاة المرء في بيته، إلا الصلاة المكتوبة

"you must pray inside your homes, for the best prayer of a man is what he offers in his home, except the obligatory prayer"[69]

Given the strong determination of the *Sahaba* (may Allah (swt) be pleased with them) to pray, they used to make a (special) room for prayers inside their homes where they would pray voluntary prayers and sometimes obligatory prayers (when needed) due to illness or any reason that would prevent them from praying in a mosque. Bukhari has named a chapter in his book (Chapter: About (taking) the mosques in the homes and Bara' bin Aazib (ra) prayed in the mosque at his home collectively). Under this chapter, Bukhari mentioned the story of Itban bin Malik al-Ansari al-Badri,

---

[68] Transmitted by Muslim (h/730). For more about praying in house, please refer to "Houses in the light of Quran and Sunnah / Zaid (Page 227 -228)
[69] Bukhari (h/731) and some other places and Muslim (h/781) from Zaid bin Harith, may Allah be pleased with him.

may Allah (swt) be pleased with him, that he visited the Prophet Peace be upon him and said,

يا رسول الله، قد أنكرت بصري وأنا أصلي لقومي، فإذا كانت الأمطار سال الوادي الذي بيني وبينهم فلم أستطِع أن آتي مسجدهم فأصلي بهم، وودت يا رسول الله أنك تأتيني فتصلي في بيتي فأتخذه مصلى...، وفي نهاية الحديث: فأتاه النبي r ومعه أبو بكرt ، فقال: أين تحب أن أصلي من بيتك؟ فأشار له عتبان إلى ناحية من البيت، فصلى رسول الله به ركعتين...

"O Allah's Messenger, I have weak eyesight, and I lead my people in prayers. When it rains, the water flows in the valley between my people and me, so I cannot go to their mosque to lead them in prayer. O Allah's Messenger Peace be upon him! I wish you would come to my home and pray in it so that I could take that place as a Musalla (place to worship), and at the end of the hadith, it says that the Prophet Peace be upon him and Abu Bakr, may Allah (swt) be pleased with him, visited his home, and the Prophet Peace be upon him asked, "where do you like me to pray in your home?", Itban pointed to a place, and the Prophet Peace be upon him lead them in two *raka'hs* of prayer...."[70]

Here we turn our call towards parents and educators: Pray in your homes (other than obligatory prayers), for it has (various benefits, including) sincerity, upbringing, building homes with the *Dhikr* of Allah, teaching the ignorant, reminding the negligent, brining angels, and chasing the devils and similar great benefits.

---

[70] Bukhari (h/425) and some other places, Muslim (h/33) from Mahmood bin Rabi', may Allah be pleased with him.

For the woman, there is no doubt that her prayers (obligatory and voluntary) in her home are better, most secure, and most covering (her modesty). The Prophet Peace be upon him also guided women and said

صلاة المرأة في بيتها أفضل من صلاتها في حجرتها، وصلاتها في مخدعها أفضل من صلاتها في بيتها

"it is more excellent for a woman to pray in her home than in her courtyard, and more excellent for her to pray in her private chamber than in her home.)[71] Albeit, the woman is not prevented from (praying) in a mosque (don't stop Allah's women slaves from going to Allah's mosques)[72],

however, without (wearing) adornments and without bringing any evil for her or for others.

As for the couple's prayer during the night is concerned, it is enough for them to be included among the men and women who (frequently) remember Allah.[73]

ورحم الله رجلًا قام من الليل فصلى وأيقظ امرأته فصلت، فإن أبت نضح في وجهها الماء، وكذلك المرأة

---

[71] Transmitted by Abu Dawud (h/570) from Ibn Masud, may Allah be pleased with. Albani graded it "Sahih" in Sahih al-Jami' (2/713)

[72] Transmitted by Bukhari (h/900) and at some other places, Muslim (h/442) narrated from Ibn Umar. May Allah be pleased with them

[73] Transmitted by Abu Dawud (h/1309) and Ibn Maja (h/1335) from Abu Sa'id Khudri and Abu Hurayrah, may Allah be pleased with them. Albani graded it "sahih" in Sahih al-Jami' (1/122).

"May Allah (swt) have mercy on a man who stood from his bed during night and prayed and woke his wife and she prayed, and if she refused, he sprinkled (drops of) water on her face, and so did the woman"[74]

It is a Sunnah to greet with *"Assalam o Alaikum"* when entering the home. Allah (swt) says

﴿.. فَإِذَا دَخَلْتُم بُيُوتًا فَسَلِّمُوا عَلَىٰ أَنفُسِكُمْ تَحِيَّةً مِّنْ عِندِ اللَّهِ مُبَارَكَةً طَيِّبَةً ۞ ﴾..

"However, when you enter homes, greet one another with a greeting ʿof peace ʾ from Allah, blessed and good"   [TMQ An-Nur-61]

The Prophet Peace be upon him also instructed Anas, may Allah (swt) be pleased with him, as has been narrated, he said

يا بُني إذا دخلت على أهلك فسلم فتكون بركة عليك وعلى أهل بيتك

"'O my little son! When you enter upon your family then give the Salam,(for) it will be a blessing for you and upon the inhabitants of your home"[75]

Here (we see) a warning which is neglected. *Siwak* (cleaning teeth with a wooden stick) is Sunnah for prayer, which purifies the mouth in order to seek the pleasure of Allah. At times, it is neglected in places and cases out of prayer, such as when getting

---

[74] Transmitted by Abu Dawud (h/1450) and Nasai' (h/1610) and the wording belongs to both of them, and Ibn Maja (h/1336) from Abu Hurayrah, may Allah be pleased with him. Albani graded it "sahih" in Sahih al-Jami' (1/657).

[75] Narrated by Tirmidi (h/1698) and said it is "hasna ghareeb." Albani graded it "Da'eef in Da'eef al-Jami' (1/926).

up (from sleep) during the night, for the fasting person, and when making *Wudu* (ablution). However, what is absent or neglected mostly is doing Siwak when entering the home. Muslim transmitted from Aisha, may Allah (swt) be pleased with her, she said,

كان رسول الله إذا دخل بيته بدأ بالسواك

"Whenever Allah's Messenger Peace be upon him entered his home, he used tooth-stick first of all"[76]

The wisdom behind, as has been said by Qurtubi, that is perhaps it was due to the Prophet (Peace be upon him) used to start with voluntary prayers, he rarely used to offer voluntary prayers in the mosque; therefore, the Siwak would be for the voluntary prayer.

Others say

:الحكمة في ذلك أنه ربما تغير رائحة الفم عند محادثة الناس، فإذا دخل البيت

كان من حسن معاشرة الأهل إزالة ذلك

The wisdom behind that could be that the smell of the mouth sometimes changes when speaking to people, so when he (Peace be upon him) entered the home, it was part of the good companionship with the wife to remove that smell.[77]

---

[76] Sahih Muslim (h/253)
[77] Commentary by al-Suyuti on Sunan an-Nasa'i (1/31)

4. Qur'an is (guidance), (light), (enlightenment), (remedy), and book of Allah, (its rope is flawless), (its way is straight), and (it is mercy for all worlds):

The Ahl ul Qur'an (those who recite and follow Qur'an) are the most blessed. The homes in which Qur'an is recited during the day and the night are the most beautiful ones (along with those homes in which) the letters (the face) are counted. They increase their good deeds (reward) tenfold. You will see that reciting one part of the Qur'an has more than five thousand good deeds (rewards).

So, we could imagine the case of the one who recites more than that. Know that the favour of Allah (swt) is great upon the one who recites Qur'an.

The favour of Allah (swt) is great upon the one who established *Tarbiyyah* (Nurturing) in the homes by disseminating the recitation of the Qur'an among young and old, men and women. (Morning and Evening) Qur'an units established inside mosques or floors dedicated for women have great virtue, after Allah's grace, in the Qur'anic echoes of household members like the echoes of honeybees, as they memorize, revise, and reflect upon (the meanings of the Holy Qur'an). However, parents must exert their efforts towards the Qur'anic recital inside their home.

Many Prophetic *Ahadith* mention the virtue of reciting the Qur'an and its **effects in the home in general or (the virtue of) some specific Qur'anic chapters and *ayaat*.** Muslim narrated in his book that Hudair said

بينما هو ليلة يقرأ في مربده (موضع في بيته) إذ جالت فرسه، فقرأ ثم جالت

أخرى، فقرأ ثم جالت أيضًا، قال أسيد : فخشيت أن تطأ يحيى(ابنه)فقمت

إليها، فإذا مثل الظُّلَّة فوق رأسي فيها أمثال السُّرج عرجت في الجو حتى ما أراها، فغدوت على رسول الله فأخبرته بذلك، فقال: تلك الملائكة كانت تسمع لك، ولو قرأت لأصبحت يراها الناس ما تستتر منهم

"That one night he recited the Qur'an in his enclosure, when the horse began to jump about. He again recited and (the horse) again jumped. He again recited, and it jumped as before. Hudair said: I was afraid lest it should trample (his son) Yahya. I stood near it (the horse) and saw something like a canopy over my head with what seemed to be lamps in it, rising up in the sky till it disappeared. I went to the Messenger of Allah (swt) Peace be upon him on the next day and brought him the news. Upon this, the Messenger of Allah (swt) Peace be upon him said: Those were the angels who listened to you; and if you had continued reciting, the people would have seen them in the morning, and they would not have concealed themselves from them.[78]

Do we not wish Angels casting their shadows over our homes while we recite the Holy Qur'an in them? Another narration says,

فإنها السكينة تنزلت عند القرآن، أو تنزلت للقرآن

"it is *Sakinah* "serenity" that lands when reciting Qur'an or lands for Qur'an."[79]

And who would not desire the "*Sakinah*" landing on his home?

---

[78] Bukhari (h/5018) and Muslim (h/796), the words here belong to Muslim.
[79] Transmitted by Bukhari (h/3614) and some other places, Muslim (h/795).

Do you know that Qur'an contains nothing of small (value)? The first verse of the chapter of Ikhlas

$$﴿قُلْ هُوَ ٱللَّهُ أَحَدٌ ١﴾$$

"Say, ˹O Prophet,˺ "He is Allah—One ˹and Indivisible˺""   [TMQ Alikhlas:1]

 is equal to one-third of the whole Qur'an. The Prophet Peace be upon him said

أيعجز أحدكم أن يقرأ في ليلة ثلث القرآن؟ قالوا :كيف يقرأ ثلث القرآن؟ قال :

قل هو الله أحد تعدل ثلث القرآن

"Is it difficult for any of you to recite one-third of the Qur'an in one night? The companions said, how is that possible? The Prophet Peace be upon him answered, (قل هو الله أحد) is equal to one-third of the Qur'an"[80]

When you teach your children the chapter of al-Fatiha, it is the greatest chapter of the Holy Qur'an and the seven oft-repeated *ayaat* (Al- Mathaini) and is the Great Qur'an.[81] Qurtubi said,

اختُصت الفاتحة بأنها مبدأ القرآن وحاوية لجميع علومه

---

[80] Bukhari (5015), Muslim (h/811-812). Al-Mazri said: Quran has three types (of content): stories, rulings, and the characteristics of Allah, and Surat al-Fatiha is specific to the characteristics, thus is one part of the three parts (Abdul Baqi's note on Muslim) (1/566).

[81] Bukhari (h/5006) and some other places from Abu Saeed bin al-Mua'lla, may Allah be pleased with him.

"Surat al-Fatiha has been distinguished for being the tenet of the Qur'an and contains all of its sciences.[82]

ومن قرأ الآيتين من آخر سورة البقرة في ليلة كفتاه

He who recites the two *ayaat* at the end of Surat Al-Baqarah at night, they will suffice him.[83]

It is said,

أجزأتاه عن قيام الليل بالقرآن، وقيل أجزأتاه عن قراءة القرآن مطلقًا داخل الصلاة

أو خارجها، وقيل: كفتاه بإذن الله من كل سوء، وقيل غير ذلك

"They will reward him equal to standing the whole night in prayer and that they will reward him equal to reading Qur'an totally inside or outside Salah (prayer). It is also said that the two *ayaat* will protect him from every evil, and like wise"[84]

One should be keen to learn and recite Surat al-Baqara in homes for it protects from devils, with the permission of Allah. Muslim narrates that

أن الشيطان ينفر من البيت الذي تُقرأ فيه سورة البقرة

"Devil runs from the home in which Surat al-Baqara is recited"[85]

---

[82] Fathul Bari (9/54)

[83] Bukhari (h/5009) and Muslim (h/708)

[84] Fathul Bari (9/56)

[85] Sahih Muslim (h/780) and it also transmits (Recite Surah al-Baqara, for to take recourse to it is a blessing and to give it up is a cause of grief, and the magicians cannot confront it, hadith number 804). It has been known from

Oh *Murabbi* (educator), it is worth it that you make your family members memorize Ayat al-Kursi.

فمن أوى إلى فراشه وقرأ آية الكرسي لم يزَل عليه من الله حافظ، ولا يقربه شيطان

حتى يُصبح

"Whenever someone went to his bed, recited the Verse of "Al-Kursi" for then a guardian from Allah (swt) will be guarding him, and Satan will not approach him till dawn"[86]

وعوِّذ نفسك وأهل بيتك بالمعوذتين (الناس والفلق)، فما تعوَّذ متعوِّذ بمثلهما

Make yourself and your family members take refuge in *Mu'awwizatain* (Al-Falaq and An-Nas), for they are the best *ayaat* in which a person seeking refuge can take refuge.[87]

The Prophet Peace be upon him used to protect Hasan and Husain, may Allah (swt) be pleased with them, by *Mu'awwizatain*.

In any case, reciting Qur'an in homes brings "Sakinah" and chases away devils.

The practical procedures that help in reciting Qur'an in homes include the following:

---

some righteous servants of Allah that they used to recite Surat al-Baqarah frequently and they confirmed observing its effects.
[86] Bukhari (h/3275).
[87] Transmitted by Ahmad in his Musnad (h/21189) from Ubayy ibn Ka'b, may Allah be pleased with him. Abu Dawud (h/1463) from Aqba bin Amir, may Allah be pleased with him. Albani graded it "sahih" in Sahih al Jami' (1/1316).

a.   Establishing Qur'an recitation and reflection units inside homes.

b.   Establishing competitions in Qur'an memorization or Qur'an interpretation and reflection.

c.   Taking help of older children for encouraging and stimulating (the interest of) young children.

d.   Choosing audio Qur'anic library with a number of reciters so that family members can assess their reading and enjoy Qur'an through their beautiful voices.

e.   Reading an easy Qur'anic interpretation in order to understand the meaning

5.   **Awrad (*Adhkar* – remembrance of Allah) in Morning and Evening:**

Wird (*Dhikr*) is a fence that protects, with the permission of Allah, the human being from the Satan (both from the humans and the djinns) and protects the home and the family.

The Murabbi (Educator - male or female) must be keen to do the *Wird* by himself, teach it to his family so they can read them in the morning and evening with persistence. The Sunnah has brought us a number of Hadith that should be recited in the morning and the evening, these include:

- Reading Ayat al-Kursi and the last (*ayaat*) of the Surat al-Baqara
- Surat al-Ikhlas and Mua'wwazatain (thrice)

- اللهم بك أصبحنا (أمسينا)...

- أعوذ بكلمات الله التامات من شر ما خلق (thrice)

- Sayyid al-) اللهم أنت ربي لا إله إلا أنت خلقتني وأنا عبدك إلخ
(Istighfar

- (hundred times) سبحان الله وبحمده

- (ten or hundred times) ...لا إله إلا الله وحده لا شريك له

- لا حول ولا قوة إلا بالله

- (hundred times) سبحان الله، والحمد لله، ولا إله إلا الله والله أكبر

And other *Adhkar* and *Wird* that bring calmness and happiness to hearts and by which Allah (swt) protects from the deceits of the devils.

It is important to read one or more books on *Adhkar* such as (Al-*Adhkar* lin-Nawawi) or (Hisnul Muslim by Qahtani) or others to understand the *Adhkar* and their virtues. *Adhkar* can be downloaded on mobile for ease of reading at any place.

6. (Setting) a Good Example in the home:

Sometimes humans hear from their eyes rather than their ears as long as the act is more powerful than the word. A good example relieves educators from many things. The establishment of following the example of the Prophet Peace be upon him is a *Shari'* approach and a divine order

$$﴿لَّقَدْ كَانَ لَكُمْ فِى رَسُولِ ٱللَّهِ أُسْوَةٌ حَسَنَةٌ لِّمَن كَانَ يَرْجُواْ ٱللَّهَ وَٱلْيَوْمَ ٱلْأَخِرَ وَذَكَرَ ٱللَّهَ كَثِيرًا ﴾﴿٢١﴾$$

"Indeed, in the Messenger of Allah, you have an excellent example for whoever has hope in Allah (swt) and the Last Day, and remembers Allah (swt) often" [TMQ Al-Ahzab – 21];

Therefore, it is worth for the parents to get closer to this picture (of the Prophet Peace be upon him) and become an excellent example for their children in their homes in the worship and behaviours. The parents are, in Salah (prayer) and praying it properly, in speaking truth, investing their time, and dealing with others with good, an excellent example for their family members. They are in each of their affairs and cases, an excellent example. The Prophet, Peace be upon him, has taught the woman to be a perfect example in dealing with her child from a young age and guided her to be true in her dealing. Abdullah bin Amir, may Allah (swt) be pleased with him, narrates that My mother called me one day when the Messenger of Allah (swt) Peace be upon him was sitting in our home. She said: Come here, and I shall give you something. The Messenger of Allah (swt) Peace be upon him asked her: What did you intend to give him? She replied: I intended to provide him with some dates. The Messenger of Allah (swt) Peace be upon him said: If you were not to give him anything, a lie would be recorded against you.[88]

The parents are a true mirror for their boys and girls, and often they imitate their manners.

---

[88] Transmitted by Abu Dawud in the Chapter of General Behavior (h/4991) and Musnad Ahmad (h/15702). Albani graded it "hasan" in Sahih al-Jami' (1/282).

It is a disgrace for the educator to say what he does not do and that his behaviours are in total contrast to his guidance and advice. It is a mistake for the educator (including parents) to think that he can hide something, of his wrong behaviour, from the people of his home.

The extent that should be avoided is that the parents or one of them are plagued by misery/bad habit, while they dislike it and is keen to get rid of it at the earliest. However, before getting rid of it, he attempts not to export it to others. He, thus, hides it and does not show it, not because of hypocrisy rather due to being embarrassed on the one hand, and, on the other hand, due to the eagerness that no one from his family should get familiar with it, nor should he become a reason for inflicting someone else with this misery.

Making an excellent example by performing the *Shari'* obligations, avoiding the forbidden things, and adopting good traits, eases the way of *Tarbiyyah* (Nurturing) for parents and cuts short the stretches of advice, reminding, and warning, although being necessary.

It is known and renowned that there is love in souls towards imitating and copying. Hence the Prophet Peace be upon him who is the most truthful, said,

الرجل على دين خليله فلينظر أحدكم من يُخالل

The man follows the religion of his friend, so one should see who he makes his friends.[89]

Therefore, we should understand the extent of the impact of the parents with whom the children spent most of their time permanently.

7. **Understanding between Spouses about the Roles of the *Tarbiyyah* (Nurturing):**

Tarbiyyah (Nurturing) is a collection of guidance and behaviours. It is important that parents integrate with the ways of the *Tarbiyyah* (Nurturing), they should understand each other and not run away, and they should integrate. Each of them has a task and method. If the mother has an inclination for (tenderness) and (gentleness) with her children at a time, the father then, must represent the role of (firmness) and (seriousness) so that the tenderness is not missed, the seriousness is not lost, the firmness perishes, and (thus) the anarchy prevails.

The parents must come to terms with the method of *Tarbiyyah* (Nurturing) for their children. Their approaches should include the carrot and stick approach, commanding and preventing, firmness and softness, encouraging and stimulating, and similar influential strategies. They should not appear contradictory but rather integrating roles. It is also important that the disputes between the spouses should not come to light, their voices should not go up, and their difference should not highlight. These affect children negatively and reflect on the effect of *Tarbiyyah* (Nurturing).

It is fitting that humans tend to make mistakes, and the dispute could happen between the spouses. A similar thing has happened in the home of the Prophet Peace be upon him, and there are still disputes occurring in the homes of the people. However, the spouses should be keen, as much as possible, to hide that and resolve their problems before they come into the knowledge of their children. If these things come into the light and the family members become aware of them, then (the spouses should adopt) the path of turning back by making reconciliation and compromise in the witnessing and presence of the children. This will eliminate the effect and repair the damage.

It is essential that kind behaviour prevail in the home, and the spouses should urge each other on that.

فما كان الرفق في شيء إلا زانه، وما نُزع من شيء إلا شانه

Kindness in anything adds to its beauty, and its absence in anything makes it defective.[90]

وإذا أراد الله عز وجل بأهل بيت خيرًا أدخل عليهم الرفق

And when Allah (swt) intends good for a household, he introduces kindness in them.[91]

The spouses should also conform to the behaviour of modesty as

فما كان الفحش في شيء قط إلا شانه، ولا كان الحياء في شيء قط إلا زانه

---

[90] Muslim (h/2594)
[91] Transmitted by Ahmad in Musnad (h/24427). Albani graded it "sahih" in Sahih al-Jami' (1/117)

"*Al-Fuhush* (obscenity) is not present in anything, but it mars it, and *Al-Haya'* (modesty) is not present in anything, but it beautifies it."[92]

The repulsion of the spouses and frequent disputes and fighting spreads chaos and damages homes. It creates a charged environment that inherits anxiety and delusion for the children and calls them to slip from the home and look for another environment where they might find peace and assurance. They rejoice by coming out of the home, while perplexity and sadness covers them when they enter it. Such homes drive away (the children) and do not impart *Tarbiyyah* to them. The spouses are a cause of this by their frequent in-fighting and differences. How can such spouses bring together the *Tarbiyyah* (Nurturing) methods while they are in such a state?

Hence, the man and woman being aware of their roles in *Tarbiyyah* (Nurturing), their convergence, understanding one another, and making the *Tarbiyyah* (Nurturing) of their children a common purpose, each helps in the (process) of *Tarbiyyah* and assists in producing a righteous generation, with the permission of Allah.

8. Supplication for the Household Members:

Supplication (asking for help from Allah) is a (form of) worship for Allah (swt) in general. It is a demand in order to seek the righteousness of the offspring and the family members. When the man uses the possible means for *Tarbiyyah* and then raises his hands towards heaven, asking his Lord for guidance and success,

---

[92] Transmitted by Tirmidhi (h/1974) and Ibn Maja (h/4185). Albani graded it "sahih" in Sahih al-Jami' (2/987)

there remains no doubt that he is handing over his matter to the one who owns the guidance and the success. Whenever the supplication is true and sincere without any violation in the act of asking, its chances of being accepted become higher. Allah (swt) says

﴿وَقَالَ رَبُّكُمُ ٱدْعُونِي أَسْتَجِبْ لَكُمْ إِنَّ ٱلَّذِينَ يَسْتَكْبِرُونَ عَنْ عِبَادَتِي سَيَدْخُلُونَ جَهَنَّمَ دَاخِرِينَ ۝﴾

{call upon me and I will respond to you} (Ghafir – 60).

He also says:

﴿وَإِذَا سَأَلَكَ عِبَادِي عَنِّي فَإِنِّي قَرِيبٌ أُجِيبُ دَعْوَةَ ٱلدَّاعِ إِذَا دَعَانِّ ۝﴾..

"When My servants ask you ˹O Prophet˺ about Me: I am truly near. I respond to one's prayer when they call upon Me"

[TMQ AlBaqarah:186]

He (swt) further adds:

﴿.. فَلْيَسْتَجِيبُوا لِي وَلْيُؤْمِنُوا بِي لَعَلَّهُمْ يَرْشُدُونَ ۝﴾

"So let them respond ˹with obedience˺ to Me and believe in Me, perhaps they will be guided ˹to the Right Way˺"

[TMQ Al-Baqarah – 186]

It means that they obey me and testify to it.[93]

While interpreting this verse, Qurtubi mentioned several things that prevent the supplication from being responded to. He also mentioned some conditions for (the supplication) to be accepted and the (best) times for acceptance.[94]

The parents must realize that their supplication, provided that it is undertaken with sincerity, truthfulness, and without infringement, falls within the (list of) supplications that are not rejected. The Prophet Peace be upon him said:

ثلاث دعوات يستجاب لهن، لا شك فيهن :دعوة المظلوم، ودعوة المسافر، ودعوة

الوالد لولده

"There are three supplications that will undoubtedly be answered: the supplication of one who has been wronged; the supplication of the traveller; and the supplication of a father for his child."[95]

Correspondingly, the supplication of the father for his child is answered: (there are three supplications that will undoubtedly be answered of which includes the supplication of the father for his child.)[96]

The parents, therefore, should stick to making supplications for their children and be aware of calling down evil on them, especially when in a state of anger, as it might be the time in which

---

[93] Tafsir Tibri (2/166)
[94] Al-Jami' li Ahkam al-Qur'an (2/309-313)
[95] Transmitted by Ibn Majah (h/3862). Albani graded it "hasan" in Sahih al-Jami' (1/582)
[96] Transmitted by Tirmidhi (h/1905)

Allah (swt) is to confer upon them what they demand. Regarding this matter, the Prophet Peace be upon him said

لا تدعوا على أنفسكم ولا تدعوا على أولادكم، ولا تدعوا على خدمكم، ولا تدعوا على أموالكم، لا توافقوا من الله ساعة يُسأل فيها عطاء فيستجاب لكم

Don't curse your own selves, nor your children, nor your belongings. There is the possibility that your curse may synchronize with the time when Allah (swt) is about to confer upon you what you demand, and thus your prayer may be readily responded to.[97]

The parents should make supplication for their children with persistence, and their supplication should not be concerned with the good of the worldly life only. This, even being legitimate and required, the supplication for their righteousness and being upright is more important. The prophets, peace be upon them, used to pray for their children, and their supplications included:

﴿رَبِّ ٱجْعَلْنِي مُقِيمَ ٱلصَّلَوٰةِ وَمِن ذُرِّيَّتِى ۚ ..﴿٤٠﴾﴾

"My Lord! Make me and those 'believers' of my descendants keep up prayer"   [TMQ Ibrahim – 40]

﴿.. قَالَ رَبِّ هَبْ لِى مِن لَّدُنكَ ذُرِّيَّةً طَيِّبَةً..﴿٣٨﴾﴾

"My Lord! Grant me—by your grace—righteous offspring"

[TMQ Ali'-Imran – 38]

---

[97] Transmitted by Muslim (h/3009) from the hadith of Jabir, may Allah be pleased with him.

﴾ ۞ .. وَأَصْلِحْ لِي فِي ذُرِّيَّتِيۤ .. ۞(١٥)﴿

"And instill righteousness in my offspring"   [TMQ Al-Ahqaf – 15]

Praying for children formed a characteristic of the righteous people. Fudayl Ibn 'Iyad, may Allah (swt) have mercy on him, made supplication for his child (Ali) and said:

اللهم إني اجتهدت أن أودب عليًّا فلم أقدر على تأديبه فأدبه أنت لي

My lord, I exerted my effort to teach the manners to Ali and I did not succeed, so you teach him the manners for me.

 Allah (swt) answered his call and (Ali) became one among the Awliya (great servants of Allah), devoted to Allah, and having great standing, as has been said by Al-Dhahabi.[98]

In our times, many *Murabbi* (Nurturers) complain of delinquency among their children, and it was supplication that relieved them. Allah (swt) made their offspring righteous. This is advice for parents (both father and mother) not to be subsided and not to lose hope for their offspring becoming righteous while applying all the possible means in *Tarbiyyah*. They should look for the time in which the supplication is answered, present their hearts, choose comprehensive prayers, and consider the manners of making a supplication (such as praising Allah (swt) first, then sending the salutations on the Prophet Peace be upon him in the beginning and the ending.)

---

[98] Siyar A'lam al-Nubala (8/390-392)

9. Focusing on the *Tarbiyyah* of the elder children and making them participate in the (process of) *Tarbiyyah* (Nurturing):

No matter how distinct the role of the father and the mother with children is, they need the assistance of their children in the *Tarbiyyah* of their brothers. Therefore, paying attention to the elder children (male or female), caring more about them, and using them later by making them participate in guiding and Tarbiyyah of their brothers, is a successful and experimented matter. It also relieves the responsibility of the parents and helps in the *Tarbiyyah*, and why is that? Because the elder among the children often becomes an excellent example for those who come after him, and the language of the brother with his brother and of the sister with her sister is more impactful.

There is no doubt that the age difference or convergence of age has an effect on the *Tarbiyyah*. Encouraging the older son (or daughter) to carry his role of seeking the righteousness of those who are younger than him further reforms him, expands the scope of responsibility, and is like an early training for Da'wah and *Islah* (calling and reforming). It also carries a future goal, which is to prepare them for their future family and their role in their future homes. The family is a small nucleus of the society, and whenever the families increase in numbers, and the good and righteousness prevail in them, it becomes an indication of good and the sign of the righteousness of the society. The bigger society is nothing but a group of small families.

Here, the fathers and mothers must make further efforts to enlighten their elder sons and daughters. They should spend the time and effort when needed to support them in the (process of) *Tarbiyyah*. Giving confidence to them is important. Training them on the good, accompanying them to the sessions and visits of *Khayr* (meetings), providing them with the beneficial knowledge, culturing them, and informing them of their presence, all these help in their *Tarbiyyah* (Nurturing) and qualify them to participate in raising those who are younger than them.

10. Important people in *Tarbiyyah* (Nurturing):

If the parents or one of them complains of the weakness of *Tarbiyyah* and having less impact in their family members for any reason, they should then seek help, after Allah, from those who are influential, possess knowledge, and are in charge of *Tarbiyyah* (Nurturing), outside home, and these include:

a. The Imam of the local mosque. He is entrusted with the responsibility of the followers of the mosque. When the guardian of the family seeks his help in reforming the home and puts before him some problems in order to seek guidance and the right advice, the Imam should feel the responsibility and assist in reforming the homes of his locality to the possible extent by legitimate means which he feels are appropriate, such as visitation, guidance, awakening desire in the mosque, proposing competitions, and urging learning the Holy Qur'an, etc.

b. The orator of the Friday sermons, who is closer to home, is the second who should be consulted. The orator should provide assistance in the *Tarbiyyah* (Nurturing) and reforming homes with his distinct sermons and his beneficial programs for the locality, and encouraging the youth (male and female) on doing good and warning them from the evils and the strife.

c. The School teachers are a primary pillar in *Tarbiyyah* (Nurturing). Our sons and daughters spend a great deal of time in their schools. Perhaps the student (male and female) hear from their teachers more than what they hear from their parents. So, can the role of the teacher (male and female) be estimated (outside school)?

The reality and the experience indicate that many families became righteous, young boys became upright, and the young girls found the right path due to the guidance of the Imam or by hearing a beneficial sermon or the impact of the male or female teacher. *Tarbiyyah* (Nurturing) is a group of interconnected units that complement each other.

In the Muslim community, all are invited to cooperate with one another in goodness and righteousness

﴿ى.. وَتَعَاوَنُواْ عَلَى ٱلْبِرِّ وَٱلتَّقْوَىٰ وَلَا تَعَاوَنُواْ عَلَى ٱلْإِثْمِ وَٱلْعُدْوَٰنِ وَٱتَّقُواْ ٱللَّهَ إِنَّ ٱللَّهَ شَدِيدُ ٱلْعِقَابِ ۝ ﴾

"Cooperate with one another in goodness and righteousness and do not cooperate in sin and transgression. And be mindful of Allah. Surely Allah (swt) is severe in punishment"

The impact and results of making someone righteous are great, as

لأن يهدي الله بك رجلًا واحدًا خير لك من أن يكون لك حُمْر النعم

If a single person achieves righteousness (embraces Islam) at your hands (i.e., through you), that will be better for you than the red camels."[99]

d. The righteous friend influences his friend. Therefore, choose friends of sons and daughters carefully. A bad company destroys the companion. Ask about the company of the child, and notify that

﴿ٱلۡأَخِلَّآءُ يَوۡمَئِذِۭ بَعۡضُهُمۡ لِبَعۡضٍ عَدُوٌّ إِلَّا ٱلۡمُتَّقِينَ ٦٧﴾

"Close friends will be enemies to one another on that Day, except the righteous" [TMQ Az-Zukhruf – 67]

The Prophet Peace be upon him said:

ومثل الجليس الصالح والجليس السوء كحامل المسك ونافخ الكير

"The example of a good companion (who sits with you) in comparison with a bad one is like that of the musk seller and the blacksmith's bellows (or furnace)."[100]

---

[99] Bukhari (h/2942) and some other places, Muslim (h/2406).
[100] Bukhari (h/2101) and at one another place, Muslim (h/2628).

The parents enquiring about the friends of their sons and daughter helps significantly in their Tarbiyyah. In contrast, there are many boys and girls who got lost because of the bad company. You need to imagine the impact of the bad companions in comparison with the intelligent and smart, so what would be the case with the inexperienced fools. In the story of the demise of Abu Talib and his sad ending, the Prophet Peace be upon him visited and said to him:

يا عم، قل لا إله إلا الله، كلمة أحاج لك بها عند الله، فقال أبو جهل،

وعبد الله بن أبي أمية :يا أبا طالب، أترغب عن ملة عبد المطلب؟ وأبى

أن يقول لا إله إلا الله

O uncle! Say: None has the right to be worshipped except Allah, a sentence with which I will defend you before Allah." On that Abu Jahl and `Abdullah bin Abi Umaiya said to Abu Talib, "Will you now leave the religion of `Abdul Muttalib?, and he refused to say, "none has the right to be worshipped except Allah."[101]

Given the impact of sitting and being in the company of the bad on a personality like Abu Talib, we should be mindful of the impact of the bad company on those who are lower than him (in terms of mind and thought).

---

[101] Bukhari (h/4772) and Muslim (h/24).

Mechanisms and Tools for *Tarbiyyah* (Nurturing) in Homes

In order to achieve the goals of *Tarbiyyah* (Nurturing), and to reach the effect of its contributing factors, we need several mechanisms and means that would invoke the desire of sons and daughters and attract their attention, and make them accept the guidance with welcoming hearts and satisfied souls. The beauty of content in guidance and *Tarbiyyah* (Nurturing) also needs the beauty of the heart that bears it and the means that executes it.

The guide should not disregard anything of the good. He should also take into account the diversity and variability of psychics and moods as much as possible. These mechanisms and means include the following:

1. The Good Word:

فالكلمة الطيبة صدقة

The good word is charity.[102]

وتبسمك في وجه أخيك صدقة

Smiling at the face of your brother is a charity.[103]

---

[102] Transmitted by Bukhari (h/2989) and one another place. Muslim (h/1009).
[103] Transmitted by Tirmidhi (h/1956) and its original hadith is in Muslim (h/702) and at one another place for the one who wishes to see.

Speaking the good is required by *Shari'ah* and in terms of acceptance and intellect.

$$\text{﴿وَقُل لِّعِبَادِى يَقُولُواْ ٱلَّتِى هِىَ أَحْسَنُ ...﴾}$$

"Tell My 'believing' servants to say only what is best" [TMQ Al-Isra – 53]

$$\text{﴿... وَقُولُواْ لِلنَّاسِ حُسْنَا ...﴾}$$

"Speak kindly to people" [TMQ Al-Baqarah – 83]

Being uncivil and harsh, as well as limited usage of words that open up hearts and delight the ears, are lead to defect in *Tarbiyyah*.

It is a mistake for parents to imagine that their children at home don't need the best words that are selected for others outside the home. There is a guiding light in the prophetic guidance for all educators, including parents.

$$\text{فلم يكن النبي سبابًا ولا فاحشًا، ولا لعانًا}$$

The Prophet Peace be upon him was not one who would abuse (others) or say obscene words, or curse (others).[104]

When there is frequent abusing, cursing, and usage of obscene words, then it does not conform to the prophetic guidance, and we could only assume the aggravation of personality, division, and dispersion. Parents should choose the most beautiful phrases by

---

[104] Transmitted by Bukhari (h/6031/6046) from the hadith of Anas bin Malik, may Allah be pleased with him. Also refer to Mawsooa' Sahih Ahadith Shama'il al-Nabawiyah by Dr. Humam and his son Mohammad, Page 161.

which to address their children. This brings them closer, makes them realize confidence, and instils love in their hearts.

Since children, especially the young ones, are most likely to make mistakes and (since they) frequently move, and sometimes (cause) unprompted damage, the parents must tolerate and forgive that and use good words. We must reflect upon the guidance of the Prophet Peace be upon him when a child (Hasan or Husain), may Allah (swt) be pleased with them, urinated in his lap, Umm Fadl, may Allah (swt) be pleased with her, (who was breastfeeding him) hit him on the shoulder. Prophet Peace be upon him said:

أوجعت ابني رحمك الله

"you have hurt my son; may Allah (swt) have mercy on you."[105]

Verily the best words include what encourage and stimulate. When you address your son, saying,

"Oh noble, hey hero, hey honourable, hey chivalrous, hey intelligent,"

And similar beautiful phrases, they draw future pictures for him. And when you speak to your daughter, saying:

"O beautiful, O blessed, chaste, tenacity, righteous, you have taste and beauty",

And similar things, you also draw pictures of tranquility & happiness (Sa'adah) and open good future prospects.

---

[105] Narrated by Ibn Majah and graded "sahih" by the author of Mawsooa' Sahih Ahadith Shama'il al-Nabawiyah, Page 162.

The best words also include giving dignified and beautiful nicknames to sons and daughters like the names of the prophets, peace be upon them, the companions of the Prophet, Peace be upon him or those who came after them, or the names of scholars and nobles. This gives them confidence, which is a good omen. Choosing a good name for the child (male or female) is the right of the children to be fulfilled by their parents.

Did you know A good word *(Kalimah Tayyibah)* may sometimes create a great future? Imam Al-Dhahbi (the great scholar) says about himself that what instilled the love for the science of hadith in me was that my Shaikh (Al-Barzali) told me one day:

خطُّك يُشبه خط المحدِّثين

"your handwriting is similar to the handwriting of the scholars of hadith."

His words inspired me and made me fall in love with the science of hadith.

Imam Al-Dhahbi was one of the great and genius scholars of the science of hadith.[106]

You could imagine the great impact of the word that is spoken by the Prophet Peace be upon him; he (Peace be upon him) speaks words and (makes) supplication that have their own impacts. He Peace be upon him said to Abdullah bin Mas'ood, may Allah (swt) be pleased with him:

---

[106] Ad-Durar al-Kaminah by Ibn Hajar (4/287).

إنك لغلام مُعلم

"you are a learned boy."

Ibn Masud says:

يقول ابن مسعود :فأخذت عنه سبعين سورة ما نازعنيها بشر

 I learned seventy suras from the prophet, and no one disputed me over them."[107]

Ibn Abbas, the great interpreter of the Quran, may Allah (swt) be pleased with him, Allah (swt) benefited him by the words and supplications of the Prophet Peace be upon him who said

اللهم علمه الكتاب

O Allah! Bestow on him the knowledge of the Book, Qur'an[108]

and another narration transmitted by Muslim, says,

اللهم فقهه

May Allah (swt) grant him a deep understanding of religion.[109]

2. Family Assembly:

---

[107] Transmitted by Ahmad (h/4412) and Ibn Hubban (h/6504). Albani graded it "hasan" in Ta'leeqat al-Hassan (10/159).
[108] Bukhari (h/75).
[109] Transmitted by Muslim (h/2477). For more, please refer to "Adab al-Mu'amla fi al-Sirah al-Nabawiyah by Dr. Sulaiman Al-Odah, P. 16-24.

No matter how busy parents are, they should not excuse from allocating time to sit with the family members, talk to each other on issues that benefit (them). They should mix seriousness with humour and joke and contribute to the service of homes. If they conduct a session of the Qur'an or the Sunnah, or the Prophet's biography (*Seerah*), at a fixed time with an agreed program, it would be something great, useful, and beneficial.

Parents should hear concerns, problems, and future ambitions from their children and share solutions and motivations.

Parents mustn't think it is a waste of time or the acts of leisure time, but rather consider it as a duty. It is a better investment in their children. When parents are convinced that investing in offspring and family is one of the greatest investments and projects that deserve attention, it invites them to choose the best time to sit with them and select the content of the conversation and the topics of the sessions.

One of the causes of anomaly and loss is that parents imagine that their main mission is to ensure food and clothing, preparing meals, and (providing) diverse foods.

That, with its importance and the need, is not the end of responsibility. The food of the spirit (*Ruh*) and the reforming of hearts, the reform of the twisted behavior, and instilling of the concept of comprehensive slavery to Allah (swt), are more important and greater (duties).

The steps for reform, change, and the call for good should start from home. It is a pity that some people sometimes (exert their) efforts in advocacy (towards the right path) and reform outside their homes, while their own homes complain of ignorance, loss, and deviation?

It is a flaw in thinking if a preacher aspires to bring change in the world while his own home remains outside the circle of his thinking or has some kind of weakness that he is able to overcome.

The Muslim man should set his priorities and start with the closest relatives (they are the first ones to have the right over good). If every Muslim cared for his home and reformed (*Islah*) the affairs of his family and offspring, the whole Muslim Ummah would be reformed. Every member of society and Ummah bears his responsibility. Our homes are the first forts, which our enemies have been and are still betting to bring corruption into them and deviate their dwellers (from the right path).

Therefore, we must pay attention to our homes and organize a session or sessions (meetings) for our families.

What is experimented and successful in continuing this session for sons and daughters even after their marriage is to make a session a week, where they meet over food or coffee and talk to each other. It is a good thing (for strengthening the) bond and (is) a righteous project.

Muhammad Peace be upon him, who is our role model, and whose responsibilities were greater than ours, for he is the (mercy to the whole universe) and has been sent to all people; still, you will find him (being) an example in taking care of his home and edifying his family, sitting with them, and even serving them. The mother of the believers 'Aishah (may Allaah be pleased with her) reveals the position of the Prophet in his home. She says:

كان يكون في مهنة أهله- تعني خدمة أهله -فإذا حضرت الصلاة خرج إلى الصلاة

He used to keep himself busy serving his family; if there happened to be prayer time, he would go out and pray.[110]

In another narration, she says:

كان يخيط ثوبه، ويخصف نعله، ويعمل ما يعمل الرجال في بيوتهم

"He sewed his clothes, repaired his footwear, and did what men do in their homes."[111]

These are the excellent characteristics of the prophets; peace be upon them: humbleness, (staying) away from luxury and self-humiliation so they will be imitated and lest they go into the reprehensible leisure. Allah (swt) says

﴿وَٱصْبِرْ عَلَىٰ مَا يَقُولُونَ وَٱهْجُرْهُمْ هَجْرًا جَمِيلًا ۝﴾

"And leave to Me the deniers—the people of luxury—and bear with them for a little while" [TMQ Al-Muzzammil – 10] [112]

However, the perfect concept that the scholars have drawn from the hadith

ثلاثة لهم أجران ...ورجل كانت عنده أمة فأدبها فأحسن تأديبها...

---

[110] Transmitted by Bukhari (h/676 and 6039) and is found at some other places.
[111] Narrated by Muslim (h/24903). Albani graded it "Sahih" in Sahih al-Jami' (2/886).
[112] Fathul Bari by Ibn Hajar (10/461).

(Three (people) have two rewards... a master of a woman-slave who teaches her good manners and educates her in the best possible way (the religion)...).[113]

Ibn Hajar said:

الأَمَة (بالنص، وفي) الأهل (بالقياس، إذ الاعتناء بالأهل الحرائر في تعليم فرائض الله وسنن رسوله آكد من الاعتناء بالأَمَة

The hadith text carried the word (a woman slave) and the (family/wife) by analogy, as taking care of the free family in teaching the duties commanded by Allah (swt) and the Sunnah of His Messenger is more emphasized than paying attention to the woman slave.[114]

Therefore, a person sitting at home and teaching his family good should be delighted with the double rewards.

3. Hosting the best people in homes:

With the effort of the man in his home, in teaching his family, he gets two rewards as has been mentioned above; it is (also) lovely to host people of goodness, scholars, preachers, and those who have experience in (the domain of) homes, in order to benefit from their knowledge and experiences.

"Visiting each other" among Muslims is (a sign) of goodness and (achieves) reward. The hadith says

---

[113] Bukhari (h/97) and at some other places. Muslim (h/154).
[114] Fathul Bari (1/190).

حقت محبتي للمتزاورين فيَّ

My love for those who visit each other in my (faith) becomes true.[115]

In another hadith, the Prophet Peace be upon him said:

من عاد مريضًا أو زار أخًا له في الله ناداه منادٍ أن طبت وطاب ممشاك وتبوأت من الجنة منزلًا

"Whoever visits the sick, or visits his brother in Allah (swt) (faith), a caller calls out: 'May you have goodness and livelihood be good, and may you dwell in an adobe in Paradise."[116]

A (righteous man's) visit to the home may become a cause of bliss and reform, and sons and daughters may listen more to the righteous (visitor) than what they hear from their parents.

It is *Mustahab* (desired) that righteous and God-fearing people visit our homes, as has been said by the Prophet Peace be upon him:

لا تصاحب إلا مؤمنًا ولا يأكل طعامك إلا تقي

Associate only with a believer, and let only a God-fearing man eat your meals.[117]

---

[115] Transmitted by Ahmad (h/22002) and Ibn Hibban (h/577). Ibn Hajar graded its chain of narration as "good" in Fathul Bari (10/500). Albani graded it "Sahih" in Sahih al-Jami' (2/796).

[116] Transmitted by Tirmidhi (h/2008) and Ibn Majah (h/1443). Alabani graded it "Hasan" in Sahih al-Jami' (2/1091).

[117] Transmitted by Abu Dawud (h/4832) and Tirmidhi (h/2395). Albani graded it "Hasan" in Sahahi al-Jami' (2/1226).

We have also been warned from the frequent visits of bad people into homes in the hadith:

مثل الجليس الصالح والجليس السوء كمثل صاحب المسك وكير الحداد ...إلى قوله :وكير الحداد يحرق بيتك أو ثوبك أو تجد منه ريحًا خبيثة

"The example of a good companion (who sits with you) in comparison with a bad one, is like that of the musk seller and the blacksmith's bellows - till the words of the Prophet Peace be upon him- that the bellows would either burn your body or your clothes, or you get a bad nasty smell thereof."[118]

All people warn about the burning of good homes, but only a few of them realize the burning of values and the corruption of morality by unscrupulous people.

The owner of the home should thus seek that righteous people visit his home and sit with his family and children according to the codes and etiquettes of Islam.

How impactful is the supplication that was made by Nuh peace be upon him

﴿رَّبِّ ٱغْفِرْ لِي وَلِوَٰلِدَيَّ وَلِمَن دَخَلَ بَيْتِيَ مُؤْمِنًا وَلِلْمُؤْمِنِينَ وَٱلْمُؤْمِنَٰتِ وَلَا تَزِدِ ٱلظَّٰلِمِينَ إِلَّا تَبَارًا ۝٢٨﴾

---

[118] Bukhari (h/2101) without the words of (it will burn your house). Albani graded it "sahih" with this word in Sahih al-Jami' al-Saghir (5829)

"My Lord! Forgive me, my parents, and whoever enters my home in faith, and ˹all˺ believing men and women. And increase the wrongdoers only in destruction"   [TMQ Nuh – 28]

It is beneficial if the visit of the righteous people is coordinated and reminded in advance, such as if the visitor talks about good morals that the owner of the home wants to establish in his household members or the opposite of it such has ill morals which he wants the people of his home to warn about, or (if he wants) to encourage on a general good or prevent from any vice. The owner of the home should check that the talk of the righteous guest is spontaneous and not forced in order to make sure that the people of the home do not feel dictated and obligatory.

In any case, everyone is more aware of his home and what they need. Wisdom is required, as is compassion.

The Prophet Peace be upon him used to visit the homes of his companions, may Allah (swt) be pleased with them.

أن رسول الله زار أهل بيت من الأنصار فطعم عندهم طعامًا، فلما أراد أن يخرج

أمر بمكان من البيت فنُضح له على بساط فصلى عليه، ودعا لهم

Bukhari and Muslim narrate that the Messenger of Allah (swt) visited a household among the Ansars, and he took a meal with them. When he intended to leave, he asked for a place in that home for him, to pray so a mat sprinkled with water was put, and he offered prayer over it and invoked for Allah's Blessing upon them (his hosts).[119]

---

[119] Bukhari (h/6080) and Muslim (h/660).

Ibn Hajar says that the hadith confirms that visiting is desired (*Mustahab*), and the visitor should make supplication for those whom he visited and with whom he ate food.[120]

This prophetic Sunnah (visiting homes) was followed by the companions of the Prophet Peace be upon him after him. There are several visits (by *Sahaba*) and the guidelines that are worth reflection and consideration.

آخى النبي صلى الله عليه وسلم بين سلمان وأبي الدرداء ، فزار سلمان أبا الدرداء، فرأى أم الدرداء متبذلة فقال: ما شأنك قالت: أخوك أبو الدرداء ليس له حاجة في الدنيا، فجاء أبو الدراداء فصنع له طعاماً، فقال له: كل فإني صائم، قال: ما أنا بآكل حتى تأكل، فأكل، فلما كان الليل ذهب أبو الدرداء يقوم فقال له: نم، فنام، ثم ذهب يقوم فقال له : نم، فلما كان من آخر الليل قال سلمان: قم الآن: فصليا جميعاً، فقال له سلمان: إن لربك عليك حقاً، وإن لنفسك عليك حقاً، ولأهلك عليك حقاً، فأعط كل ذى حق حقه، فأتى النبي صلى الله عليه وسلم فذكر ذلك له، فقال النبي صلى الله عليه وسلم "صدق سلمان

Bukhari transmits that the Prophet Peace be upon him made a bond of brotherhood between Salman and Abu Ad-Darda.' Salman paid a visit to Abu Ad-Darda' and found Um Ad-Darda' dressed in shabby clothes and asked her why she was in that state. She replied, "Your brother Abu Ad-Darda' is not interested in (the luxuries of) this world." In the meantime, Abu Ad-Darda' came and prepared a meal for Salman. Salman requested Abu Ad- Darda' to

---

[120] Fathul Bari (10/500)

eat (with him), but Abu Ad-Darda' said, "I am fasting." Salman said, "I am not going to eat unless you eat." So, Abu Ad-Darda' ate (with Salman). When it was night and (a part of the night passed), Abu Ad-Darda' got up (to offer the night prayer), but Salman told him to sleep, and Abu Ad- Darda' slept. After some time, Abu Ad-Darda' again got up, but Salman told him to sleep. When it was the last hours of the night, Salman told him to get up then, and both of them offered the prayer. Salman told Abu Ad-Darda', "Your Lord has a right on you, your soul has a right on you, and your family has a right on you; so you should give the rights of all those who has a right on you." Abu Ad- Darda' came to the Prophet Peace be upon him and narrated the whole story. The Prophet Peace be upon him said, "Salman has spoken the truth."[121]

There are many benefits and pearls in this hadith. This place may not suffice to explain all that. However, it contains the importance and legitimacy of making visits between brothers (brothers for the sake of Allah) and blood brothers being more rightful. The hadith also points out giving advice and making aware those who are lost, and the permissibility of preventing from establishing *Mustahab* (desired) things in the presence of the fear that they may lead to weariness, discontent, and missing the compulsory and required rights. It also indicates the permissibility of speaking to an alien (*non-Mahram*) woman in cases of need.[122]

We are more in need of visiting and giving advice to each other and being reminded of the rights of the family and the offspring.

---

[121] Bukhari (h/1968).
[122] For more refer to: Fathul Bari by Ibn Hajar (4/209-210).

4. The Purposeful Visits

Besides visiting the household members, what contributes to their comfort and cheerfulness, and brings joy to their hearts is visiting those who love socializing with them and benefitting from (the qualities) that they possess, especially if the time of the visit is chosen and those who are to be visited. They may return from their visit with benefits that were not found in their own home and may come out of the visit sending more praise to Allah (swt) and thanking Him, as they may find that those they have visited have less furniture or have a narrow living place; thus they thank God for what he has blessed upon them.

A Muslim, when visiting others, must adhere to the etiquette of the legitimate visit. If he sees good, he remembers Allah (swt) and fills with joy for his Muslim brother, and if he sees the opposite to that, he thanks Allah (swt) and invokes Him for the betterment of his brother. He does not abuse, disparage or reveal any secret. Hence the visits lead to their desired purpose.

A person must choose whom he will visit like he chooses who visits his own home. You may visit either the one who would have a better living standard and in which case you will benefit from him, or the one who will have a lower standard of living in comparison to you, and in that case, you will help him and thank God for the blessings he has bestowed upon you, or he could be having a living standard just like you, and in such case, you will enjoy each other's company and advise each other for sticking to the truth and remaining patient.

It is essential that our visits are purposeful, and strive for reward and virtue away from backbiting and slandering.

As we must keep our tongues safe, we must also keep our eyes safe as well from looking into the privacy of the people and things which they would not like to be looked at. The ears should be kept safe from hearing that is forbidden, such as music and means of forbidden fun, or extending the discussion about the honour of the people and making them the subject of meetings. In such cases, these would be negative visits and meetings that do not bring any good.

Our honorable *Shari'ah* wants safe and reassuring homes to be visited in order to achieve good and rewards, and (it wants you) to visit in order to benefit, help and earn the reward.

Our *Shari'ah* doesn't want homes that are Repelling. These are the homes in which the household members feel distressed and weary, either because of the abundance of the things that are prohibited in Islam, or for the poor treatment by parents, or the poor relationship with the brothers, or any other reasons that make the homes a place of expulsion and not a place of stability. These homes must address their situation, consider the reasons why their sons and daughters run away from them, address their problems, and provide viable alternatives.

There are important and programmed visits, those agreed upon by the visitor and the one being visited, such as memorizing something from the Qur'an, or reading beneficial books, or having competitions and prizes. The atmosphere of visits and competition among those with similar (traits) creates an atmosphere of motivation and gives visits a sense of importance. So, let's make sure (conducting) such visits and choose their programs carefully.

5. Entertaining and Beneficial Journeys:

The journeys (carry with them) a breather and many benefits.

The household members should travel to refresh, rejuvenate, and as a reward for the efforts they have put, and to move in the vast kingdom of God.

However, these trips achieve their purpose more when parents or older brothers take an interest in them. The objectives of these trips are: to visit a relative for fostering good relations with the kin, or a true friend to strengthen the relationship with him, or to walk in the vast areas of land to ponder upon and reflect.

﴿أَفَلَا يَنظُرُونَ إِلَى ٱلْإِبِلِ كَيْفَ خُلِقَتْ ۝ وَإِلَى ٱلسَّمَآءِ كَيْفَ رُفِعَتْ ۝ وَإِلَى ٱلْجِبَالِ كَيْفَ نُصِبَتْ ۝ وَإِلَى ٱلْأَرْضِ كَيْفَ سُطِحَتْ ۝﴾

"Do they not ever reflect on camels—how they were ˊmasterfullyˋ created;} {and the sky—how it was raised ˊhighˋ;} {and the mountains— how they were firmly set up;} {and the earth—how it was leveled out?"
[TMQ Al-Ghashiyah – 17 – 20]

It is important that those in charge of the journey draw the attention of their children towards the creation of the sky, the stars, and the galaxies, and to the land and the mountains, lowlands, valleys, plains and rivers, and seas... all testifying to Allah's greatness and His power. These gestures could be more appropriate while on a journey than in (in a) stable (place) and within cities.

When the purpose of the journey is to visit holy places, such as the two Holy Mosques (*Al-Haramain al-Sharifain*), then it is a light and obedience (of Allah); (it allows the opportunity to) remind the travellers of the virtue of the visit, the reward of praying in *Al-Haramain*, and the etiquette of mosques. Among the favours of Allah (swt) upon us is that our country, the Kingdom of Saudi Arabia, comprises plains and the mountains and has cold and hot weather areas, and the roads connecting them are active and wide, and above that, we have summer resorts and parks that the visitor is proud to visit when they are preserved and (equipped with) fully integrated services.

This is in addition to the presence of the two Holy mosques and the effects that surround them that remind us of our great history and the Jihad of our Prophet Peace be upon him and his companions; may Allah (swt) be pleased with them.

There is a kind of trip that is experimented and (has been found to be) successful. It is to allocate a trip for young people of the same age group for they are in need of the trip and picnic more than others. It is important that the father sometimes accompanies his children on a road trip that includes some kinds of entertainment and sports programs along with some benefits and guidance. On such trips, young people discover themselves, get closer to their father, their talents come out, and are trained on various types of services, which they will need later in their life, such as the public service skill, preparing food, or (making) coffee, the etiquette of the companionship and mingling (with others), and other meanings and goals that are achieved by such trips. Whether the trip is carried in the land or other places that are worth visiting, it brings pleasure and reassurance and it is enough that it mingles father with his children and is an opportunity for the children to get closer and cooperate with each other. It is experimented with and quite successful even in the case of the children having different mothers. We should thus make sure to pay attention to such trips and use them and make our children happy with them. Other young people who are close to them or the sons of our friends about whom we feel assured can also participate in such trips so that the cross-fertilization of ideas is achieved.

Cooperating over good with each other is a great thing.

Regarding the trip programs, it is good to choose nice and light items on the road and on board the vehicle. It would be great to start with the Qur'an (recitation) to achieve the blessing, correcting the errors, and make the recitation better.

The programs to be undertaken during the journey could be light competitions, encouraging prizes, hearing useful audio clips, *Samar* conversations (poems written by Samar al-Dasouqi) or permissible poems and songs that bring pleasure and give the trip an atmosphere of enjoyment and benefit. Travellers carrying small and valuable leaflets and distributing them to those who would benefit from them would be an embodiment of *Da'wah* in the trip. It is useful to remember Allah (swt) (carry out *Dhikr* - remembrance) during the journey and to remember and repeat some *Adhkar* having great rewards that are easy to repeat to save (oneself) from the boredom of the long journey on the one hand, and also to make *Dhikr* of Allah (swt) a slogan of the traveller, (on the other).

It is important to remind here the etiquette of travelling, including the prayer to be recited at the start of the journey as well as organizing the responsibilities and services during the trip so that some people do not bear the burden (of the whole journey) while some are neglected.

It is also important to train boys and girls on serving (others) while travelling. These journeys may become (like training) courses for them, given the scarcity of these courses or being rare in homes.

Household members taking a journey is an opportunity to foster trust, create beneficial initiatives and competitions, (are a chance of) renewing the lifestyle, and (provide an opportunity to) inhale the fresh air in the wilderness, villages, abandoned places, and cities.

The journey should be accompanied by thanking and remembering (Allah). The Sunnah of the Prophet Peace be upon him during the travelling, and its etiquettes should be learned. The travellers should realize that Allah (swt) is watching over them and is with them wherever they are.

Note What Allah (Swt) says:

أَلَمْ تَرَ أَنَّ ٱللَّهَ يَعْلَمُ مَا فِى ٱلسَّمَٰوَٰتِ وَمَا فِى ٱلْأَرْضِ مَا يَكُونُ مِن نَّجْوَىٰ ثَلَٰثَةٍ إِلَّا هُوَ رَابِعُهُمْ وَلَا خَمْسَةٍ إِلَّا هُوَ سَادِسُهُمْ وَلَآ أَدْنَىٰ مِن ذَٰلِكَ وَلَآ أَكْثَرَ إِلَّا هُوَ مَعَهُمْ أَيْنَ مَا كَانُواْ ثُمَّ يُنَبِّئُهُم بِمَا عَمِلُواْ يَوْمَ ٱلْقِيَٰمَةِ إِنَّ ٱللَّهَ بِكُلِّ شَىْءٍ عَلِيمٌ ۞

"Do you not see that Allah (swt) knows whatever is in the heavens and whatever is on the earth? If three converse privately, He is their fourth. If five, He is their sixth. Whether fewer or more, He is with them wherever they may be. Then, on the Day of Judgment, He will inform them of what they have done. Surely Allah (swt) has ˹perfect˺ knowledge of all things"

It is also important here to realize the value of supplication while travelling. Supplication made by the traveller is one of the supplications that are answered (by Allah). We should remind ourselves as well as our colleagues about that.

6. Home Library:

Learning the sciences of *Shari'ah* is of great virtue and high ranking. Allah (swt) says:

$$\text{﴾..يَرْفَعِ ٱللَّهُ ٱلَّذِينَ ءَامَنُواْ مِنكُمْ وَٱلَّذِينَ أُوتُواْ ٱلْعِلْمَ دَرَجَٰتٍ ..﴿}$$

"Allah (swt) will elevate those of you who are faithful, and ˹raise˺ those gifted with knowledge in rank" [TMQ Al-Mujadila – 11]

Angels lower their wings in approval to the one seeking knowledge.[123] People having knowledge cannot be equal to those who do not have knowledge.

Without neglecting other sciences, we should form a small library that is filled with selected books to keep them available for household members to read, research, and earn a deep understanding of the religion of Allah. It is appropriate if the library contains books that are fit for young and old, male and female. This will generate a love for reading and seeking knowledge among them as well as turn their leisure time into something useful.

---

[123] Narrated by Tirmidhi (h/2682), Nasai' (h/158), and Ibn Majah (h/223). Albani graded it "Sahih" in Sahih al-Jami' (2/1079).

Having a register in the library to record the visitors and readers and giving prizes to the frequent readers to further encourage them would stimulate the usage of the library.

The library stimulants also include choosing its location, the attractiveness of its furniture, the clarity of lighting to facilitate reading and familiarization, and diversity of the sciences (Interpretation of the Holy Qur'an, Hadith, Biography of the Prophet Peace be upon him, History, Literature, Stories, Aqidah (Islamic Creed), Jurisprudence, Biographies), and similar sciences that that will formulate ideas, purify souls, and answer the questions.

Sometimes it would be possible to conduct the family meeting in the library. It is also nice that the parents or one of them present a case for discussion and refer the children to the library to accustom them to doing research and review. Above all, the library book must be selected in a language that is understandable and has a beautiful print.

The library should not be devoid of entertaining and useful stories and books and competitions that activate the mind and help in reading. There should also be a specified space inside the library for audio recordings, such as the recordings of the Qur'an in beautiful recitations, lectures or seminars, and meaningful dialogues, as some people (like) listening more than reading.

It has been observed that some homes contain many forbidden images or pieces of furniture that exceed the usage, while there is no library and book, even if a modest one. Therefore, we should pay attention to the items of our homes and should not spend too much on one thing while completely neglecting the other thing.

7. Mobile Messages and Family Groups:

Mobile has now become an integral part of the life of human beings irrespective of their age or gender. It also poses a risk and threatens the *Tarbiyyah* (which will be discussed later). This device can be used as a tool and means for *Tarbiyyah* (Nurturing) in homes through the following:

a. Creating (groups) for family members in which they communicate with each other. Influential content in *Tarbiyyah* should be chosen (and shared in the group). The group represents a link for the family, through which they advise, congratulate, and communicate with each other while travelling or residing.

b. There are several private or general messages which the parents can send through these groups to their sons or daughters, carrying special advisory for a member or having a general message for the whole group. These are *Tarbiyyah* (Nurturing) messages with nice phrases that make the family members feel the tenderness of parenthood and the guidance from the parents. We should use the messages over "mobile" as a means and space to express more than confronting. These messages are also experimented with and have an impact on the *Tarbiyyah* (Nurturing); we should thus use these "mobiles" for that purpose.

c. Purposeful programs can be downloaded on the "mobile", foremost of which is the Holy Qur'an and some of the interpretation of its *ayaat*, as well as other useful programs that the family can download and benefit from to be a valid alternative to the programs that deviate (from the right path).

d. "Mobile" can also be used as an alarm for prayer times, especially the prayers before which a person remains asleep.

e. It is essential that using "mobile" should not last for a longer period of time. There should be continuous awareness about the importance of time and not waste it on mobile and on things that are not useful. The harmful things should be warned of besides remaining cautious about getting involved in them. Using "mobile" should not be at the expense of other programs and duties. However, if it distracted from the obligatory prayers, this would be a dangerous indicator, and parents should quickly fix that.

f. Mobile can also be used, in case of parents or one of them or even children travelling to follow them and to know their wellbeing. This also includes awakening them to (pray) Fajr prayer and asking about their situation in general so that they feel the presence of parents with them even if they are relieved and travelling.

8. Developing Skills for both Genders:

In order for our sons and daughters to understand the issues of *Tarbiyyah* (Nurturing), it is necessary to advance their ambitions and develop their skills. The shaping of the Islamic creed (*Aqeedah*) is essential for the young people to protect them from the deviations of polygamy (*shirk*) and the foolish acts of (*Bid'ah*). Correcting the belief (*Mo'taqad*) is a prerequisite for any acts being accepted (by our Lord).

Intellectual skills should also be developed, and perceptions of the authentic culture should be expanded so that the individual doesn't become prey to destructive ideas and gets threatened by novel and alien thoughts.

There are skills and values that parents must consider developing in their children. The skill of the relationship with others, the etiquette of dialogue, and the methods of influencing and getting influenced, all create the ability to socialize with others and benefit from their positivity among the children. It also saves them from the foolish imitation, getting drawn into any presentation (idea), or admiring any shine, albeit at the expense of their values and morals.

The emotional building is also important so that the relationship between the educators (*Murabbi*) and those whom they educate is not just a formal relationship devoid of any emotions, which makes boys or girls (girls are more in need of the emotion) be carried away by undesired emotions in which get drawn for their lack of availability in the home environment.

And the reality testifies to the fact that sometimes the girl may fall "prey" to deceptive words of love and tenderness and may have an emotional vacuum; thus, she accepts it, and it may lead her to things that she hates. Therefore, the educators should use affectionate words, passionate emotions, and gentle feelings with their children so that they are not deceived by others and get along with you and listen to your directives.

Observing the guidance of the Prophet Peace be upon him and his (method) of educating his family members, especially the young ones, we find him (Peace be upon him) being simple, having jokes, and treating them kindly is quite evident. The children loved him during his presence with them, and whenever he returned from his travels, they were happy to see him.

كان رسول الله إذا قدم من سفر تُلُقِّيَ بصبيان أهل بيته

Muslim narrates that when Prophet Peace be upon him came back from a journey, he met the children of his household.[124]

Aqra bin Habis saw Prophet Peace be upon him kissing Hasan ibn Ali (may Allah (swt) be pleased with him) and said,

إن لي عشرة من الولد ما قبَّلتُ منهم أحدًا، فنظر إليه رسول الله ثم قال: من لا يرحم لا يُرحم

"I have ten children, and I have never kissed anyone of them," the Messanger of Allah (swt) (Peace be upon him) looked at him and said, "whoever is not merciful to others will not be treated mercifully."[125]

---

[124] Muslim (h/2428).
[125] Bukhari (h/5997) Muslim (h/2318).

Then there are skills that are gender-specific that he/she needs most. To give a few examples, if a girl needs the skills of housekeeping and taking good care of it, let us help her succeed in her future home. A young man needs the skills of trading, ways of Halal earning, and making wealth that may rescue him during the hour of need; thus, we should help him succeed as well.

In any case, parents must consider building the skills needed by the generation in the present and the future. These are tools that help in the *Tarbiyyah* (Nurturing) and contribute to future successes.

9. Treating mistakes in homes

الخطأ وارد، وكل ابن آدم خطَّاء

Mistakes tend to happen and every son of Adam sins.[126]

Our homes are not dwelled by angels who do not disobey Allah (swt) in matters which He (swt) commands them. The methods that help in Tarbiyyah also include the method and how to address mistakes if they occur. Sometimes we want to treat a mistake and fall into something that is more severe than the original mistake due to the mistreatment. Parents must be courteous and understand the mistake and the method of treating it before they begin with the process of treatment.

---

[126] Tirmidhi (h/2499) Ibn Maja (h/4251). Albani graded it "Hasan" in his book Sahai al-Jami' (2/831)

Methods of Treating the Mistakes:

a. (Beware of) Publicising (How is it some people do it) so as not to embarrass and confront the sinner and give him a chance to retreat from his mistake.

b. With the insistence and repetition of the mistake, the sinner would be addressed alone in the form of advice in which expressions of affection, appreciation, and guidance would be used. He would realize the effect of the mistake and its bad repercussions. We should also use the guidance method and direct advice used by the Prophet Peace be upon him with one of his companions that benefited him. Umar bin Abi Salma narrates that

كنت غلامًا في حِجر رسول الله وكانت يدي تطيش في الصحفة،

فقال لي رسول الله :يا غلام، سمِّ الله، وكل بيمينك، وكل مما يليك .

فما زالت تلك طعمتي بعد

I was a boy under the care of Allah's Messenger (Peace be upon him), and my hand used to go around the dish while I was eating. So Allah's Messenger (Peace be upon him) said to me, 'O boy! Mention the Name of Allah (swt) and eat with your right hand, and eat of the dish what is nearer to you." Since then, I have applied those instructions when eating.[127]

c. There is a prophetic method to treat the mistake, and that serves as deterrence in an indirect way. It is to sensitize the

---

[127] Bukhari (h/5376) and Muslim (h/2022).

sinner of his mistake without talking to him, which is to (avoid) him until he returns to his senses.

إذا اطَّلع على أحدٍ من أهل بيته كذب كذبة لم يزل معرضًا عنه حتى يُحدث توبة

If the Messenger of Allah (swt) (Peace be upon him) knew that someone from his household has spoken a lie, he (Peace be upon him) would avoid him until he repented.[128]

d. The educator may sometimes need (to impose) punishment or a slight sensation of it. Some people do not benefit from Publicity, and do not respond to being avoided and abandoned, and need something serious than that, such as intimidation by punishment and knowing it about to take place. The Sunnah of the Prophet mentions that

علِّقوا السوط حيث يراه أهل البيت فإنه لهم أدب

"hang the whip where the people of the home would see it for this would teach them the manners."[129]

Although the Prophet (Peace be upon him) did not extend his hand to hit someone, even he (Peace be upon him) did

---

[128] Transmitted by al-Aqeeli in Kitāb al-ḍuʻafāʼ al-kabīr (1/9) and (4/430) and denied it. Al-Suyuti attributed it to Ahmad and Hakim, as in Saheeh al-Jami' (2/855). Al-Albaani said in Silsilat as-Sahiha (82/5). He attributed it in al-Jami' to Ahmad and Hakim from 'Aishah. I dont find it there now. al-Manawai mentioned that it has been narrated by Hakim from Ibn-Qun'ab and this has been graded "Sahih" in Sahih al-Jami'.

[129] Transmitted by Abd al-Razzaq (h/17963) and Bukhari in Adab al-Mufrad (h/1229) and Tibrani in al-Kabir (h/10671) and the wording belongs to him. Albani graded it Hasan in Sahih al-Jami' (2/744).

not offend the people of his home and servants with something that is lighter than that (such as complaining and forbidding from doing). Anas said:

خدمت رسول الله عشر سنين، فما قال لي أُفٍّ قط، وما قال لشيءٍ

صنعته لِمَ صنعته

I served the Messenger of Allah (swt) (Peace be upon him) for ten years. He never complained to me and never said about anything which I did; why have you done this?[130]

Perhaps the hanging of the whip here is intended to follow up on the etiquette and care for good manners.

e. Safe and successfully tried means include punishment by assigning the sinner with something that benefits him, such as being asked to memorize a part of the Holy Qur'an (as per his ability), or read a useful book that accommodates his style, or assigning him with certain tasks at home that are not hard, as well as that, do not lead him being gloated or disrespected by the members of the household. These and similar tasks are an optimal investment and lead to correcting the mistake.[131]

f. With all the above methods of treating mistakes (or others), the manners of (graciousness and forgiveness) must be present in the mind of the educators as it is closer to being righteous. Allah (swt) says

---

[130] Narrated by Bukhari (h/6911) and Muslim (h/2309).
[131] Fayd al-Qadir by Munawi (4/325) and Forty Advices for Transforming Homes by al-Munjid (P. 85).

$$\left\{\ ..\ وَأَن تَعْفُوٓاْ أَقْرَبُ لِلتَّقْوَىٰ\ ..\ (٢٣٧)\right\}$$

"Graciousness is closer to righteousness"

[TMQ Al-Baqarah – 237]

This has also been commanded by *Shari'ah* while dealing with children and spouses, even if they commit some kind of transgression. Allah (swt) says,

$$\left\{يَٰٓأَيُّهَا ٱلَّذِينَ ءَامَنُوٓاْ إِنَّ مِنْ أَزْوَٰجِكُمْ وَأَوْلَٰدِكُمْ عَدُوًّا لَّكُمْ فَٱحْذَرُوهُمْ وَإِن تَعْفُواْ وَتَصْفَحُواْ وَتَغْفِرُواْ فَإِنَّ ٱللَّهَ غَفُورٌ رَّحِيمٌ (١٤)\right\}$$

"O believers! Indeed, some of your spouses and children are enemies to you, so beware of them. But if you pardon, overlook, and forgive ˹their faults˺, then Allah (swt) is truly All-Forgiving, Most Merciful." [At-Taghabun – 14]

g. Sometimes overlooking and feigning ignorance become the reason for treating the mistake as the sinner realizes that his mistake was not noticed. Sometimes he regrets doing it and people not noticing his mistake helps him quit the mistake (and leads to) remorse and repentance.

(We should) differentiate between reprehensible negligence, and between overlooking and feigning ignorance of certain acts, which is a beneficial tactic and a mechanism of *Tarbiyyah*.

10. Doing justice with Children:

It is the nature of the human psyche to love one person more than another or be affectionate and closer to someone than the other. This is normal, and it may have its reasons and justifications. I here mean that the disparity in love or being close or far is something of which could also happen with the children. However, what we should be cautioned about is that it should not lead to any special attitudes, justifications, and unfairness in giving and gifting that would be at the expense of justice that is mandated by *Shari'ah* and linked with piety

اتقوا الله واعدلوا بين أولادكم

Fear Allah (swt) and be just to your children[132]

Murabbi's (Nurturers), in general, and parents, in particular, should treat children equally. They should make them realize the equity in their treatment and appreciation. They should not show any appreciation or respect to some and neglect some others, as this will (adversely) impact the Nurturing (*Tarbiyyah*) and may lead to some deviation as a result of unfairness and negligence.

This moral (justice) has been taught by Muhammad (Peace be upon him) to his companions and then to the whole Muslim Ummah. An-Nu`man bin Bashir narrates that his father (may Allah (swt) be pleased with him) took him to the Prophet (Peace be upon him) and said,

---

[132] Bukhari (h/2587) and some other places, Muslim (h/1623).

:يا رسول الله إني أشهدك أني قد نحلت النعمان كذا وكذا، فقال :أَكُلُّ ولدك

نحلت؟ قال :لا، قال :فأشهد غيري، ثم قال :أليس يسرك أن يكونوا في البر سواء؟

قال :بلى، قال :فلا إذًا

"O Messenger of Allah, I make you a witness that I have given Nu'man a gift" Prophet (Peace be upon him) said: Have you given it to every one of your sons? He replied in the negative. Prophet Peace be upon him said: then make someone else the witness to it, then said "would it not make you happy that they (your children) be equal in good? He said: why not. Prophet (Peace be upon him) said: then let it be so.[133]

We sometimes struggle with the methods of Tarbiyyah (Nurturing) and complain about the lack of positive outcomes, which could be for some reasons and constraints (that can't be explained here). However, one of the reasons could be an imbalance in doing justice, or some kind of preference for some children over some others, which we may not have felt in our daily practice, but the eyes and the hearts of the children may have felt it, and possibly it stopped them from accepting (the advice), and we did not sense it. Therefore, we should pay attention to being just and making all children realize our love and appreciation. Some children might be better than others in terms of (mentalities) or (services and goodness); still, we should not show an inferior view towards any of them. Instead, we should attach the weak children with the strong ones, and this is a great challenge and a method and mechanism in *Tabiyyah* (Nurturing), which is perhaps missed by some *Murabbi's* (Nurturers).

---

[133] See the previous Hadith

Things That Threaten Homes And The Duty Of Parents Towards It

When we identify the causes, methods, factors, and mechanisms of *Tarbiyyah* (Nurturing), we must strive to preserve these gains and protect them from negative influences, pay attention to the things that threaten *Tarbiyyah* (Nurturing), the factors of corruption that invade our homes from inside – for which we are responsible, or from outside and which we are able to drive away and counter with all our strength. These threats include:

1. **The Parents' Realization Of Their Responsibility Towards** *Tarbiyyah* **(Nurturing)**

is a major factor in *Tarbiyyah* (Nurturing), and the lack of responsibility or weakness is taking care of the children is an important element of deviation and threatens with corrupting homes. It is true that guidance and success come from Allah, but we must apply the necessary steps toward care and *Tarbiyyah* (Nurturing) as has been commanded by *Shari'ah*.

Those who fail to nurture and don't take responsibility for their daughters or sisters should contemplate how much virtue and reward they lose, which ultimately takes the *Muhsin* (caregiver/perpetrator) to Jannah. Prophet (Peace be upon him) said:

من كان له ثلاث بنات أو ثلاث أخوات، أو بنتان أو أختان فأحسن صحبتهن،

واتقى الله فيهن، فله الجنة

Anyone of you having three daughters or three sisters or two daughters or two sisters and he raises them well and fears Allah (swt) in their matters, he shall have Jannah. [134]

This has been mentioned to encourage and as a reward for those who do good and fear Allah (swt) in the matters of his household; there is also a warning for those who commit negligence. He will be asked on the day of judgment about this responsibility to which he didn't pay proper attention. Allah (swt) says

﴿يَٰأَيُّهَا ٱلَّذِينَ ءَامَنُواْ لَا تَخُونُواْ ٱللَّهَ وَٱلرَّسُولَ وَتَخُونُواْ أَمَٰنَٰتِكُمْ وَأَنتُمْ تَعْلَمُونَ ٢٧﴾

"O believers! Do not betray Allah (swt) and the Messenger, nor betray your trusts knowingly"　　　　　　　　　　　　　　　　[TMQ Al-Anfal – 27]

Is it known that the negligence in the Nurturing (*Tarbiyyah*) of children by any parent becomes a reason to take away his guardianship over his child.

There is a meaningful story that Ibn al-Qayyim narrated from his Shaikh (may Allah (swt) have mercy on them) and said: I heard our Shaikh (may Allah (swt) have mercy on him) saying, "The parents disputed with each other (over the custody) of a boy in front of some ruler. The ruler gave the boy a choice to choose between the

---

[134] Narrated by Abu Dawood and Tirmidhi as has been mentioned in Jami' al-Usool (1/413). Bukhari mentioned it in Adab al-Mufrad. Albani graded it Hasan in "Sahih Adab al-Mufrad – Page 58).

two, so he chose his father. His mother said: "Ask him why he chose his father." He said, "My mother, you sent me to school every day, and the teacher beats me, while my father lets me play with the boys.". The ruler made the decision in favour of the mother and said: You deserve him more.

Ibn al-Qayyim also narrates from his Shaikh that "if a parent does not Nurture his child and looks after his matters which Allah (swt) has made obligatory upon parents then he/she would be disobeying (Allah), and he/she shall have no guardianship over the child."[135]

Many fathers and mothers do not promote virtue and prevent from vice. For these type of people, even if they are few, the outcome of this negligence is very dangerous. There emerge young boys and girls from such homes who are unaware of the primary rulings of Islam. They do not pay attention to glorifying and worshipping Allah (swt) and leave a generation that abandons Salah and follow the desires and who is not able to bear the responsibilities and carry the duties.

These homes deprived of belief (*Iman*) and moral education often live in misery, deprivation, and suffering.

The irony is that if you were to look at these people who neglect to undertake Tarbiyyah (Nurturing) in their homes, you would find them the most capable of providing a living and caring for the health and future of their children. Should taking care of the eating, drinking, professional career, and future living be more

---

[135] Zad al-Mua'ad (5/424). Anels do not enter these houses by Ibrahim Jamal P.33).

important than caring for hearts and minds, which is the real future and the eternal life of the children?

Therefore, those who have been plagued with some negligence must question themselves and return to their senses.

2.   Access to Tools of Corruption And Not Controlling Them:

In today's world, parents are competed by other elements and means that have made their entry into the homes and have become part of its components; and if these elements and means are uncontrolled and their dangers are unattended, they will threaten homes and families.

Satellite broadcasts and enormous e-publishing have become a major threat due to their presentation of dangerous films, whether by their scenes that arouse sexual instincts, their rebellion against values, morals, and modesty, or by arousing suspicions, doubt, atheism, and infidelity. Both the trials (desires or suspicions) represent a threat to our homes and allow deviation among young boys and girls. Therefore, it is necessary to get rid of these corrupt channels and control the household members in watching and listening to these channels. We should abandon the approach of *"let them watch and get familiarised, and then the matter will end."*

It is not permissible for the guardian to provide these channels inside the home and leave teenage boys and girls becoming prey to their programs (that are carefully and professionally directed at corrupting them), which the young boys and girls will realize only after a certain period has passed. In contrast, these negative media materials would have moved through their veins, becoming part of their lives, shaping their behaviours, and influencing their future. Scientific and field studies have been published that observed the consequences of these resources, and their results are quite frightening; thus, the recommendations made by these studies should be taken into serious consideration.

Perhaps the tool of corruption could be simple but also impressive. Listening to (singing) and (vulgarity) from any device, raising the volume of the forbidden, and providing entertaining tools and musical instruments in homes make them a haven for devils.

Where is the difference then between homes in which the recitation of the Holy Qur'an is listened to frequently and between those homes in which the voices of male and female musicians and singers are mixed and in which the pictures of male and female dancers are shown, and homosexuals and nude people are presented as role models of the young from (of both genders)? Doesn't that represent a threat to Muslim homes?

I am not here discussing the ruling over "singing" and "the musical tools." I am referring only to a hadith narrated by al-Bukhari, which states that

ليكونن من أمتي أقوام، يستحلون الحِرَ، والحرير، والخمر، والمعازف

"From among my followers, there will be some people who will consider illegal sexual intercourse, the wearing of silk, the drinking of alcoholic drinks, and the use of musical instruments as lawful."[136]

I take guidance from the ruling of the mother of the believers, Aishah (may Allaah be pleased with her). The daughters of her

---

[136] Narrated by Bukhari (h/5590) مجزوما به ووصله غير واحد

brother were circumcised, and she was asked: should we call someone who will entertain them?" She said, "Yes, why not." So, they invited some singers, and Aisha happened to pass through the home and found him singing and moving his head which was filled with dense hair. She said,

أُفٍّ، شيطان، أخرجوه، أخرجوه

"Uff, a devil, remove him, remove him."[137]

However, it is essential to be aware, in general, that there is no difference between Arab or Western channels if they are similar in offering corrupt content. There are today viable alternatives, programs, and useful channels, thank Allah, that parents should benefit from, if necessary.

3. Modern Means of Communication And Their Invasive Programs:

The guardian of the home may control the entry of some channels that do not bring any good and may block some channels that could negatively influence his family and children; however, the most difficult thing is to block the means of contemporary communication, especially smartphones (mobiles). These devices have invaded homes and have become a medium of comfort for young and old, male and female, a medium of leisure, and a traveller's companion. These devices even infringe upon the times

---

[137] Narrated by Bukhari in al-Adab al-Mufrad (h/1247) and Bayhaqi in al-Sunan al-Kubra (h/21010). Albani graded it as "Hasan" in his commentary on al-Adab al-Mufrad). He noted in his book al-Silsila al-Sahiha (2/349): it's chain of narration is close to being "hasan."

of (obligatory) duties, make the viewer postpone the obligatory prayers, and neglect his daily responsibilities. The brain gets addicted to them by watching and listening to them.

The problem is that this device (mobile) carries everything from the good and the bad, has channels and suspicious sites and is filled with fake news and rumours besides containing invasive and influential programs, etc.

It is true that it contains various objective programs, and useful clips and is a good medium if used in an appropriate manner. However, that depends on controlling it and choosing the beneficial and avoiding the harmful, which is quite a challenging task. Can the father or the mother monitor the devices of their sons and daughters while they carry them all the time, and even when they go to their sleeping beds and are accompanied by these devices while they rest and while they travel.

When these devices, whatever their type and programs, pose a threat to the family (with their ability to educate, influence, reform, and spoil); the shortest way to protect from them is the frequent and in-depth awareness and its sustainability for the household members, making them aware of the consequences of its various programs, and guiding them to choose the beneficial ones, besides building the concept of being watched and monitored by Allah, and instilling good morals such as zeal and modesty among them.

Treatment and risk reduction methods include limiting the time to indulge with these devices and obliging everyone to close them at specified times. If any technique can be used to block the wrong sites once and for all, it would be better and more practical, but it is complicated. If the guardian could reduce its presence or at least not allow it until a certain age, in this case, the owner of the mobile (after reaching that certain age) would be able to distinguish between the beneficial and harmful.

However, the biggest key is prevention, surveillance, instilling fear of Allah, raising awareness of the dangers of these devices, offering useful alternatives, and making supplication for the family and the offspring.

O Guardians! do not threaten your homes from things that you realize or do not realize, and be warned that your children be raised by people other than you, who have no morality or religion, and be a good example for your household members in the ways and how to use these devices and choose its beneficial programs, and remain cautious and warn (the children) of its evils and trials. May Allah (swt) protect our homes from any misfortune.

The most beautiful and brief phrases that I have seen about the description of "Mobile" is:

هو من أخف ما يكون حِملًا ووزنًا في الدنيا، وقد يكون من أثقل ما يكون وزرًا وحِملًا في الآخرة

It is one of the lightest in terms of weight and load in Here, and could be one of the heaviest in terms of weight and load in Hereafter.

4. Drugs And Intoxicants And Their Initial Forms

Drugs and Intoxicants of all kinds are a scourge and an affliction and serious infectious diseases. They frequently disperse the peaceful homes and tear down the families. They are one of the plights of modern times and invade the minds. There are companies that also promote them, and there are also thieves and snipers, so we must remain cautious and protect our homes from them.

Rather, we should strive to protect our young children from things (that could lead them to drugs) and intoxicants, such as getting involved with smoking, as this could become the first step to storming into the world of drugs and intoxicants.

The bad companions are the most significant influencers and the path towards these diseases. Therefore, we must preserve our household members, both male and female, from the bad companions who have fallen into the calamity and want others to fall into the same. These addicts hunt boys and girls and choose certain times, such as exam days and when students come out of their school, to catch them and spoil them. We must warn our children to remain cautious of such people. We also must spread the culture of the consequences of drugs, intoxicants, smoke, and *shisha* in our homes, and how these things have badly influenced those involved with them, made them homeless, divorced, widows, deprived, poor, and dismissed from their jobs.

These drugs are the mother of all evils, and that description is enough. A man involved with such things doesn't stop there but goes beyond and indulges in *Maharim* (things that have been forbidden by Allah). It is not strange for the person addicted to drugs to (kill, fornicate, steal, and get involved with other harmful things and bad behaviours.

It is also not strange for a drug addict to abandon the obligatory worships, such as *Salah* (praying) and *Siyam* (fasting), as well as refrain from doing charity, and *Ihsan* (indulging in the acts of kindness), and other forms of worship and good behaviours.

Drugs and intoxicants first bring devastation and destruction to families, disperse and threaten homes. If the guardian of a home gets involved with such things, or any member or members indulge in such behaviours, then it is a disaster that must be urgently treated before the danger worsens.

The neighbour has a duty to reform and protecting his neighbour. The imam of the mosque must not fail in spreading the awareness and should deliver the message clearly. The school, with its teachers, supervisors, and mentors, have a major duty towards the Tarbiyyah (nurturing) of students about the dangers of drugs and its system. The government agencies involved in the fight against drugs should renew their methods of public awareness and warn, by virtue of their experience, of their types and effects. Their awareness (campaign) should reach homes, schools, mosques, and other workplaces, so that a culture of the dangers of these drugs may spread. We should reach the awareness to the degree that people start turning away from it.

يزع الله بالسلطان ما لا يزع بالقرآن

There are matters where Allah (swt) prevents by the power that can't be contained by the admonition from the Qur'an.[138]

Therefore, we must not take it the punishment of the promoters and users of these drugs lightly.

---

[138] This "athar" has been narrated from Uthman (may Allah be pleased with him) as has been mentioned in Tarikh al-Madinah by Ibn Shabbah (3/988) and the words are "ما يزع السلطان الناس أشد مما يزعهم القرآن"

Here we should pause and renew our discourse and awareness campaign:

It is good and beneficial for the school to cooperate with the anti-drug departments by bringing someone who was suffering from drug addiction and then repented from it, to express his experience and the journey of his misery because of this disease and how he started deviating in such behavior, how it ended, the effects it left on him, his family, and his reputation. He should then warn others of choosing this sinful path in a language that is simple, emotional, honest, and based on rationality.

Television programs, dialogues, and video and audio seminars can be conducted about the dangers of intoxicants and drugs and their initial forms based on the language of numbers. They should identify the risks and effects, explain the causes of the problem and its motivations, how to treat them, and raise awareness of its evils.

Awareness methods include short and warning messages over "the mobile," the inclusion of school curricula on the dangers of this disease, and prevention methods besides discussing them in the visual, written, and audio media.

It is a threat that deserves concerted efforts, an assortment of means of warning and awareness so that society does not plunge into its dangers and threaten the peaceful homes from within them.

5. Intense Anger And Despicable Conduct:

Anger is incitement to evil by Satan, a burning spark of fire, loathsome conduct, and behaviour that leads to the destruction of individuals and the dispersion of families. The Prophet (Peace be upon him) forbade from it repeatedly. He (Peace be upon him) said to the one who sought advice:

لا تغضب

"Don't be angry and furious."

The man asked the same repeatedly, and the Prophet (Peace be upon him) said in each case, "Don't be angry and furious."[139]

When anger intensifies and is accompanied by foolish behavior, it then threatens the homes and may perhaps lead to divorce and the dispersion of the family.

If it is in the nature of the man to be angry when he is made angry, especially in homes, (as) there are sometimes things that lead to anger, then the guardian of the home must control his anger, and conceal his rage. The anger should not entail actions and behaviours with dangerous consequences.

We here mention things that may help to calm the anger:

    a.   Seeking refuge with Allah (swt) from Satan, the accursed. Allah (swt) says

---

[139] Narrated by Bukhari (h/6116).

$$﴿وَإِمَّا يَنزَغَنَّكَ مِنَ ٱلشَّيْطَٰنِ نَزْغٌ فَٱسْتَعِذْ بِٱللَّهِ إِنَّهُۥ هُوَ ٱلسَّمِيعُ ٱلْعَلِيمُ ٣٦ ﴾$$

"And if you are tempted by Satan, then seek refuge with Allah. Indeed, He ʾaloneʾ is the All-Hearing, All-Knowing"

[TMQ Fussilat – 36]

In cases of anger, we must stick to these words

أعوذ بالله من الشيطان الرجيم

"I seek refuge with Allah (swt) from Satan, the accursed."

During the time of the Prophet (Peace be upon him), two people fought each other, one of them got very angry, and his jugular veins swelled. On that, the Prophet (Peace be upon him) said,

إني أعلم كلمة لو قالها لذهب عنه ما يجد (أعوذ بالله من الشيطان الرجيم)

"I know a word, the saying of which will cause him to relax if he does say it. "I seek Refuge with Allah (swt) from Satan, the accursed."[140]

b. Changing the status. If the raging person is standing, he should sit down. If it makes his anger go away else, he

---

[140] Narrated by Bukhari (h/6115) and is mentioned at some other places. It has also been narrated by Muslim (h/2610).

should lie down. This is how the Prophet (Peace be upon him) has instructed and guided us.[141]

It is better for a person with intense rage to go out of his home to any other place in order to calm himself and not to cause any wrong behavior, whether by himself or by any other person.

c. Performing ablution. If the anger and rage is an ember of fire, then the thing that extinguishes fire is water.[142]

d. The speedy recovery from anger so that the congestion does not continue, and there are no opportunities left for Satan, and the things return to their normal. The best cases of anger are (anger that comes slowly and vanishes fast).

e. The angry person should control himself. There is no strength in proving anger and the angry person leaving himself without rein. Instead, the strength and intensity lie in controlling and regulating the self. The Prophet (Peace be upon him) said,

ليس الشديد بالصُرعة، إنما الشديد الذي يملك نفسه عند الغضب

"The strong is not the one who overcomes the people by his strength, but the strong is the one who controls himself while in anger."[143]

---

[141] Narrated by Abu Dawud in his Sunan (h/4782). Albani graded it Sahih in his book Sahih al-Jami' (1/180).
[142] Narrated by Abu Dawud (h/4784). Albani graded it "Daeef" in al-Silsila al-Da'eefiya (2/52).
[143] Narrated by Bukhari (h/6114) and Muslim (h/2609).

f. Seeking the pleasure of Allah. Ibn Umar narrates,

ما من جرعة أعظم عند الله أجرًا من جرعة غيظ كتمها عَبدٌ ابتغاء وجه الله

"There is nothing that is swallowed greater with Allah (swt) in reward than a slave of Allah (swt) who swallows and contains his rancor out of a desire for the pleasure of Allah."[144]

g. It is a proven thing that the spouses should agree, in case of anger, to compete with each other for reconciliation, which is best. Neither one should refuse if the other asks. The best among them is who begins with Salam (greetings), pardons, and forgives, even if the other party has a greater fault.

6. Frequent Absence From Homes And Living In Fictitious Homes:

Staying at home after performing the required duties of religion and worldly affairs is not a flaw. The Sunnah of the Prophet (Peace be upon him) teaches us to stay at the homes in order to preserve and protect ourselves from the unhealthy things of words and deeds in gatherings that don't bring any good or meetings where there is no remembrance of Allah (swt) or encouragement for doing good and forbidding evil, or seeking knowledge or educating and calling towards good.

---

[144] Ibn Majah (h/4189) as "Marfoo". Bukhari narrated in al-Adab al-Mufrad (h/1318) as "Mauqoof". Albani in his commentary on al-Adab al-Mufrad said it is "Mauqoof", its narrators are trustworthy and is Sahih in case of "Marfoo."

The Prophet (Peace be upon him) has advised:

طوبى لمن ملك لسانه، ووسعه بيته، وبكى على خطيئته

"Blessed is one who controls his tongue, whose home is spacious enough, and who weeps for his sins."[145]

The frequent absence of the guardian from home without need is one of the factors that threaten homes, where *Tarbiyyah* (Nurturing) remains absent, monitoring of the children is less, and the mentor and the guide are missing. The family and the children need their father more, who should sit with them, be gentle with them, guide them, fulfil their needs, and monitor and refine their conduct.

There are people who take (fake) homes outside their original homes. They can be found inside restaurants, parks, or cafes, where they spend a lot of time away from their homes and the affairs of their families, doing things that are not important and, more seriously, indulging in acts that are forbidden. Sometimes sick members of their families are helped by a volunteer from neighbors, and sometimes the needs of their family members are fulfilled by someone other than their father. How can a father with such qualities undertake Tarbiyyah (*Nurture*) and reform (of his household members)?

If there is an infringement and (intellectual) assault upon the home from outside and the father or maybe the mother is far from their children, then a huge corruption could occur inside such dwellings. The children may even start venturing out of their

---

[145] Tabrani narrated in al-Awsat and Abu Na'eem in al-Hilyah. Albani graded it Hasan in Sahih al-Jami' (4/14).

homes, searching for other places where they find someone who shows kindness towards them or fulfils their needs. The size of deviation can't be imagined if such children are snatched and embraced by bad companies and environments.

Thus, the frequent travelling by parents and their absence from home creates an atmosphere of emptiness in the home and may even cause estrangement and homelessness.

In exchange for this negative behaviour, there are those who, if they are absent or travelling, even a little bit, remain connected to their homes, reassuring them, guiding them, and making them feel their presence even if they are absent.

Establishing cooperation between neighbours and the integration of their roles are positive steps. If someone is absent, the neighbour will play the role of his neighbour in terms of supervision and monitoring. In such a case, the household members would not feel the absence of their father; however, this depends on the perfect friendly terms between the neighbors and their realization of their responsibility and the neighbor's right towards them

وما زال جبريل عليه السلام يوصي محمدًا بالجار حتى ظنه أنه سيورّثه

Gabriel continued to recommend Muhammad (Peace be upon him) about treating the neighbors kindly and politely so much so that he thought he would order him to make them as his heirs.[146]

So, is it appropriate for a person that the home of his neighbour is burning and he is unaware of it?

---

[146] Bukhari (h/6014) and Muslim (h/2625).

Parents must consider sitting in their homes and with their children as Murabbi's (Nurturers) and counting it to be rewarded by Allah (swt). Our Prophet (Peace be upon him) used to serve his family in his home, mended his sandals, sewed his clothes, and worked as any man works in his home;[147] thus, he is the best example and role model for us.

7. Drivers and Servants:

They are a (blessing), who (serve), and are like (kindness), who have been (subjugated) when they perform several duties that are hard for parents. These servants have been found since ancient times. Even the homes of the Prophets, peace be upon them, had servants. In the homes of the father of all messengers, Ibrahim (Peace be upon him) and the last messenger, Muhammad (Peace be upon him), we find examples of the presence of servants. However, the danger lies when these drivers cross limits or the maid is dishonest and indulges in corrupt practices inside the home of her sponsor.

The driver may mingle with the women and commit evil and spread indecency among believers. Due to the inattentiveness of the guardians of the home about this dishonesty, he keeps fostering in the sanctuary, destroys progress and human life (offspring), and causes shame in the homes that can't be washed ever. The reason is the inattentiveness of the people of the home and the evil nature of this driver. Therefore, we must not let the driver mix with our women

---

[147] Narrated by Ahmad (h/24903). Albani graded it Sahih in Sahih al-Jami' (2/886).

فما خلا رجل بامرأة إلا كان ثالثهما الشيطان

Whenever a man is alone with a woman, the devil makes a third.[148]

We should be overconfident about our servants at the expense of our women, values, and the teachings of our religion.

The same is true with evil maids who cause rift, scourge, and problems inside homes that results in stress and anxiety. They also cause the husband and other family members to fall into the traps of adultery (may Allah (swt) forbid) and may even perform magic (such as knots, blowing into them, and the colors of magic or otherwise) that disperse the family and make them suffer in their Deen and Dunya. There are many of these maids who practice magic, and many more have killed or indulged in more shameful crimes, as has been shown by the statistics issued by the official bodies.

The owners of the homes must remain cautious and monitor and before that, choose, teach, and call the maids with good names, give them fair treatment, and fulfil their rights. They should not be assigned tasks that they can't bear, as doing so may force them to resort to retaliation in ways that would threaten the security and *Iman* (faith) of the homes.

It is not wise and reasonable for the drivers and servants to get aware of the secrets of homes. We should pay attention to honouring them and doing good with them, and not make them realize any kind of despise and inferiority.

---

[148] Narrated by Tirmidi (h/2165). Albani graded it "Sahih" in his book Sahih al-Jami' (1/499).

If the people of the home strive towards inviting male or female non-believers (servants) towards Islam or teach an ignorant man or woman that could benefit them, then it would be an excellent *Tarbiyyah* and an excellent *Da'wah* towards Islam.

8. Dispute Between Spouses And The Deviating (Behavior) Among Children:

Since understanding and cooperation between the spouses is one of the factors of *Tarbiyyah* (Nurturing), as has been mentioned previously, the frequent disputes and in-fighting hinder the *Tarbiyyah* (Nurturing) process and threaten with the emergence of delinquency among all or some children; may Allah (swt) save us from that.

This delinquency or deviation may be caused by several factors, including poor education, evil companions, the trial of lusts or obscurity, communication means and their invasive programs, etc. However, it is painful if this deviation is caused by the differences between the parents and their frequent disputes and in-fighting problems, while children listen and see and get affected by this disturbing atmosphere. The children may suffer from frustration and deterioration as parents would be unaware of their problems.

The dispute between spouses could be due to more than one reason: such as financial, psychological, false slandering, or an evil eye, or one of the spouses feeling that he/she has a right over the other which he/she did not respect, or a (second) marriage not tolerated by the first wife, or any other factors.

The spouses must be gentle and kind to each other, understand each other, and forgive and pardon one another. They should realize that the thing over which they disagree and fight is significantly less than the adverse effects that this dispute causes. They should also imagine the reward by Allah (swt) for those who restrain their anger and pardon others.

Every home has some kind of problem, and every couple falls into some dispute, at times, for we are humans. The homes of those who were better than us also suffered from similar matters. The Prophet (Peace be upon him) even intended to divorce his wives and swore an oath against them. However, these disputes were resolved. The spouses should move towards the ways and methods of resolving the conflict in order to protect themselves from *Shaitan's* temptation and protect their homes from dispersion and devastation.

Divorce should not be an option in any dispute. It is the most hateful permissible thing to Allah.[149] It is one of the factors that disperse and scatter children and possibly makes them fall into delinquency.

If the spouses find themselves unable to resolve their problems, while they themselves are the most capable of finding a solution and settling their matters, they may then choose someone who is good in his religious practices and has a sound mind to make a settlement between them or choose an intermediary from among the family of the husband and an intermediary from among the family of the wife to make a settlement between them, which is best.

---

[149] Transmitted by Abu Dawud (h/2178) and Ibn Majah (h/2018). It is Mursal as has been stated by Abu Hatim and Dar Qutni. Refer to: "al-Ilal by Ibn Ani Hatim (4/118).

When the spouses reconcile and forgive one another in the presence of their sons and daughters, they should monitor their children's life journey. If they notice a tendency towards delinquency or the early stages of deviation among any of their children, they should address it in its first steps, before the disease spreads and moves to other elements in the home, the problem grows, and threatens the reassuring homes.

9. Fault in the Home Finances:

Money is a blessing from Allah (swt) and a reason for the happiness of homes. It is money by which a man builds his home and fulfils his needs and from which the guardian feeds his parents and his children. The needs are provided for by money, and by it, a man (saves himself) from asking others.

However, that depends on reasonability in spending and moderation between overspending and miserliness. Allah (swt) says:

﴿وَٱلَّذِينَ إِذَآ أَنفَقُواْ لَمْ يُسْرِفُواْ وَلَمْ يَقْتُرُواْ وَكَانَ بَيْنَ ذَٰلِكَ قَوَامًا ۝﴾

"'They are' those who spend neither wastefully nor stingily, but moderately in between"   [TMQ Al-Furqan – 67]

Some people are involved in overspending, especially in things that are not essentials but luxuries, and soon they realize they are being buried in debts and (thus they) are left sitting destitute. Allah (swt) says:

$$ \text{﴿وَلَا تَجْعَلْ يَدَكَ مَغْلُولَةً إِلَىٰ عُنُقِكَ وَلَا تَبْسُطْهَا كُلَّ ٱلْبَسْطِ فَتَقْعُدَ مَلُومًا} $$

$$ \text{مَّحْسُورًا ۝ ﴾} $$

"Do not be so tight-fisted, for you will be blameworthy; nor so open-handed, for you will end up in poverty." [TMQ Al-Isra' – 29]

If this situation occurs, the Tarbiyyah (Nurturing) process is weakened or neglected, and things get worse, which threatens the family in terms of its material living, values, and morals. Sometimes it happens by the opposite of extra spending, which is niggardliness, miserliness, and greed that deprives children and the spouse of the least of their possible rights, resulting in another deviation. In that case, the household members may resort to asking people outside their home or put themselves in ominous things.

Since the wealth and money belong to Allah, the Muslim man and woman are responsible for this money, from where they earned it and on what they spent it. We should spend money on things that are (halal) permissible by Allah, with moderation and reasonably. The earning should also be from things that are (halal) permissible by Allah.

Here we should turn around and remain cautious. Some people indulge in Haram (things that are forbidden by Allah) in order to earn money, and they don't care about *Riba* (usury) and its dealings, while Allah (swt) has forbidden it and even threatened those who get involved with it. Allah (swt) says:

$$ \text{﴿ ... فَأْذَنُوا بِحَرْبٍ مِّنَ ٱللَّهِ وَرَسُولِهِ ... ﴾} $$

"then beware of a war with Allah (swt) and His Messenger!"

[TMQ Al-Baqarah –279]

In the modern world, there are many methods and ways of *riba*, and there are many financiers, so we must remain cautious of it as it eradicates the *Barakah* (blessing) and makes peoples and countries poor

$$﴿يَمْحَقُ ٱللَّهُ ٱلرِّبَوٰاْ وَيُرْبِي ٱلصَّدَقَٰتِ .. ﴿٢٧٦﴾﴾$$

"Allah (swt) has made interest fruitless and charity fruitful"

[TMQ Al-Baqarah – 276]

If *Riba* (dealings) becomes frequent, then its consequences cause tremor. It threatens homes from known and unknown directions. Thus we should fear Allah (swt) and give up outstanding interest. What Allah (swt) has made *halal* (permissible) is enough and sufficient from what He has made *haram* (forbidden).

The same is the case with some other *haram* (forbidden) commercial transactions that also take away blessings and threaten homes, such as fraud, cheating, deception, and collecting money from doubtful sources. Whoever falls into suspicious things may soon fall into *haram* like a shepherd who grazes (his cattle) around the sanctuary may soon transgress into the sanctuary.

Having a balance in the home expenses achieves security and happiness for the people who dwell in it, Allah (swt) willing. The things that threaten the home include imitating others, tracking the economic trends, following the demands of the careless people

$$\text{﴿وَلَا تُؤْتُوا۟ ٱلسُّفَهَآءَ أَمْوَٰلَكُمُ ..(٥)﴾}$$

"Do not entrust the incapable ˹among your dependants˺ with your wealth"

[TMQ An-Nisa – 5]

indulging in luxuries, extra spending on restaurant orders, fast food, following models in furniture and dress, expenses on foreign trips, and wasting money at parties, banquets, and events. All these and similar things are manifestations of extravagance, imbalance in the economy of household expenses that cause disequilibrium in homes and distract from other duties. Women get busy with such luxury expenses, and men are distressed with debts that have burdened them and are threatened with imprisonment or paying their debts. How can such people take care of *Tarbiyyah* (Nurturing) and save time for useful things in their homes? This wrong behaviour in expenses may lead to the dispersion of family and threaten its existence and unity. Therefore, we should be kind to each other and take a middle course. If we have wealth that exceeds our needs, we should spend it on the poor, destitute, widows, and the needy, especially on the poor found amongst our relatives. This spending is an expense that will be rewarded and compensated (by Allah). He says:

$$\text{﴿.. وَمَآ أَنفَقْتُم مِّن شَىْءٍ فَهُوَ يُخْلِفُهُۥ ..(٣٩)﴾}$$

"And whatever you spend in charity, He will compensate ˹you˺ for it"

[TMQ Saba – 39]

We should remember the fact that spending on the household members is a charity. The greatest dirham (in terms of reward) is what a man spends on his family. The Prophet (Peace be upon him) said:

دينار أنفقته في سبيل الله، ودينار أنفقته في رقبة، ودينار تصدقت به على مسكين،

ودينار أنفقته على أهلك، أعظمها أجرًا الذي أنفقته على أهلك

"A dinar you spend in Allah's way, or to free a slave, or as a charity that you give to a needy person, or to support your family, the one yielding the greatest reward is that which you spend on your family."[150]

---

[150] Narrated by Muslim (h/995) from Abu Hurayrah (may Allah be pleased with him).

The Benefits Of *Tarbiyyah* (Nurturing) In Homes

There is no doubt that homes are projects worth investing in, and putting the best efforts into nurturing their dwellers, is the greatest project and profitable trade.

Some people have stuck their ambition with the fruits and earnings of this worldly life only. However, the successful are those who seek to earn a reward in Here and Hereafter, pay attention towards the excellent *Tarbiyyah* (nurturing) of their homes that achieves fruits in both in this world and the Hereafter. Here we mention some fruits and benefits (of undertaking Tarbiyyah (nurturing) of family members):

1. Fulfilling The *Shari'* Duty:

We have been entrusted with our homes, and we are responsible for what Allah (swt) has put under our care. We will be rewarded and would be considered as those who fight in the path of Allah (swt) (even if we didn't fight with our swords/arms), if we provide excellent *Tarbiyyah* (nurturing) and strive in its methods and ways, and keep the risks and dangers away from our homes.

We commit a sin when we are negligent towards the *Tarbiyyah* (Nurturing) of our children that destroys our homes. We will be asked about this obligation that has been put upon our shoulders. A hadith narrates:

إن الله سائل كل راعٍ عما استرعاه، أحفظ ذلك أم ضيَّع؟ حتى يسأل الرجل عن

أهل بيته

"Indeed Allah (swt) will question everyone who is responsible about his charge, until the man will be asked about his family members."[151]

What will happen to a father whose son will argue against him in the courts held on the day of resurrection, and who would say: "I abandoned prayer because my father did not command me, and I did not revere the commands of Allah (swt) and the commands of his Prophet (Peace be upon him) because my father did not guide me?" What will happen to a mother whose daughter will stand against her on the day of judgment due to the negligence in her Hijab, lack of modesty, and putting men in trial, and who will say: "My mother didn't raise me (in the right direction) since my childhood?"

The responsibility of parents towards homes and the upbringing and *Tarbiyyah* (Nurturing) of sons and daughters is not a choice for us to accept or reject and fulfil or neglect. Instead, it is a responsibility and obligation. Any negligence in it will be negligence in our *Shari'* commitment, and we will realize the pain of negligence in this world and the sorrow of returning (back to *Dunya* to rectify it) in Hereafter

The reality witnessed confirms that those who undertake Tarbiyyah (Nurturing) of their homes are the happiest people

---

[151] Transmitted by Ibn Hibban (h/4493) from the hadith of Hasan al-Basri from the Prophet (PBUH). It is a "Mursal" hadith. Albani graded it "Hasan" in Sahih al-Jami' (1/365).

living in this world and the most rewarded in Hereafter. Their Lord will not leave anything (without rewarding them) in the Hereafter. Allah (swt) says:

$$﴿فَمَن يَعْمَلْ مِثْقَالَ ذَرَّةٍ خَيْرًا يَرَهُۥ ۞﴾$$

"So whoever does an atom's weight of good will see it"

[TMQ Az-Zalzalah – 7]

2. Preserving Family From Devastation:

Homes living in a state of devastation, chaos, and corruption is an indicator of poor Tarbiyyah (Nurturing) and evidence that parents are weak in their duty of caring for their home. However, caring for homes and paying attention to the *Iman* (creed), behaviour, and excellent Tarbiyyah (Nurturing) is an indicator of righteousness and evidences the awareness (among the parents).

By paying attention to our homes and giving due consideration to the *Tarbiyyah (Nurturing)* of our family members, we eliminate the opportunities of the onlookers and keep the thieves away from our homes. These thieves and onlookers are many. The homes of Muslims have been invaded only because of illiteracy, poor knowledge, and a low level of Tarbiyyah (Nurturing) and awareness.

Nothing can resist the efforts of enemies, whatever their identity or names, more than the serious integrated *Tarbiyyah (Nurturing)* that makes young and old, male and female, a line of defence in front of the hot and the evil winds of change.

If every home preserves its values and morals, understands the pride Islam (has given it), and the guardians realize their responsibility towards *Tarbiyyah* (Nurturing); the plans of enemies will not find a way to corrupt such homes.

We often complain about the abundance of corruption, the evil of those who spread corruption, and their impact on the society; however, if every owner of the home preserved and protected his kingdom (home), the corruption will not spread, and those who spread it will not succeed, the homes will not be devastated, and the children will not loose their way.

These homes and children are our kingdoms and sanctuaries whose keys are entrusted to us after guidance from Allah. An evil person can't cross its boundaries. Even if he is able to transgress into it in the dark night or when we were not looking, he will be met with the resistance for those who reside inside it have the immunity as well as the ability to resist, with the virtue of Allah, and with the good that we have instilled in them and for we have warned them against the evils and trials.

Thus, rather than making frequent complaints of the corruption, blaming those who spread the evil, killing ourselves with anxiety and sorrow, and complaining about the corruption of the times; we should instead carry our duties in our homes, as this will eliminate and protect them and will save the families from dispersion and devastation.

3. **Raising Generations That Will Bring Benefit To The Society And Ummah:**

Society is made up of a group of people, and the Ummah is made up of a group of societies. The Muslim society and Ummah is not less in the quantitative number; however, it is in dire need of the qualitative number. The marginal and superficial numbers of the Ummah do not bring any benefit to it, nor do they reform (*Islah*) the societies, fight the enemies, or resist their deception.

Tarbiyyah (Nurturing) in homes will lead to raising generations by which Allah (swt) will benefit the society and set the affairs of the Ummah in order. The righteous *Tarbiyyah* (Nurturing) creates members who are aware of their responsibilities, have a sense of their duties, and realize the dangers facing them. They push away these dangers with good and transcend the plans of the enemy with peace and security.

The societies of Muslims are in dire need of young boys and girls who have received an integrated Iman (faith) based *Tarbiyyah* (Nurturing) represented in *Ilmi* training to eliminate the illiteracy and values and morals based preparation/training to save themselves from devastation and deviation.

Indeed, our homes, when poor in *Tarbiyyah* (Nurturing), produce generations that are ready to be invaded and who surrender to the enemy. Their ambitions do not cross the boundaries of lust and (they) fall into doubtful matters.

However, the righteous home *Tarbiyyah* (Nurturing) produces positive generations that help spread knowledge and awareness. They invite (towards the right path) by their excellent behaviours before they invite by their advising speeches. The enemy counts them a thousand times, and they defeat the incoming cultures and invading values.

The homes are our first sanctuaries and the starting point from which the renaissance of the Ummah is launched, and its civilization achieves the leading role. We should, thus, reform our homes and pay attention to the *Tarbiyyah* (Nurturing) of our children. They are our biggest weapons against the devils from among Djinn and Humans and the defensive protection wall in front of the continuous evil attacks and the westernization raids from the enemies of Ummah despite their diverse religions, attributions, and tendencies.

4. The Parents Benefit In Here And In Hereafter:

The biggest beneficiaries of the *Tarbiyyah* (Nurturing) of children are the parents. Those who reform their homes are the ones who benefit from it most, with the guidance and will of Allah.

Nurturers, including parents, should not forget that children are a lifelong project that deserves utmost attention. Every contribution (made in their lives) is to be enjoyed (later). Reforming homes is a strategic objective that must have priority in our life.

A child being righteous is a thing of pride for his father and a distinctive feat for his mother. In such a case, if the parents order something, he fulfills that, and if they demand something, he brings it to them. His presence makes them happy, and when he is absent and travelling, he (remembers them in his) prayers and preserves the oath (given to them).

The righteous *Tarbiyyah* (Nurturing) produces positivity in children. They are the pillars of their parents in meeting their needs, who represent them in events, and they are relied upon in calamities and ordeals. They accompany their parents when they travel and when they rest. Their souls are happy and revered; their speech is sweet and clean, their hearts are wide and pure, unlike others who didn't benefit from the *Tarbiyyah* (Nurturing), who are struggling (live in) misery and trials, they don't fulfil any need, don't get delighted when meeting (someone) or in events. When they speak, they speak badly, their presence and absence are unnoticed, and even parents sometimes wish they remain absent, so their problems also remain absent with them. These people, even if they harm and hurt their parents, parents still keep hopes; perhaps they may wake up from their inattentiveness and return as models of (doing) good and excellent behaviour with their parents.

These are some benefits of the righteous child in Here, whereas (the rewards) in Hereafter are bigger and that shall last forever. When parents leave for the heavenly abode, the most significant thing (in terms of reward) for their afterlife, which they leave behind, is a child who prays for them. It has been narrated in an authentic hadith that "when a man dies, his deeds come to an end, except for three, that includes "a pious son, who prays for him."[152]

There is a distinctive feature of a pious son as he could be a reason for the elevation of the ranking of his father in the afterlife. It has been narrated in hadith that the ranking of the father is elevated in Jannah (heaven), and he says: How did I get this? And he is told, "because of the prayers and *Istighfar* (seeking forgiveness) by your son for you.[153]

---

[152] Narrated by Muslim (h/1631).
[153] Narrated by Ahmad (h/10610), Tabrani in Dua' (h/1249), and Al-Bayhaqi in Sunan al-Kubra (h/13459). Albani graded it "Sahih" in Sahih al-Jami' (1/334).

The righteous son is always faithful and loyal to his parents in this worldly life and in the afterlife. This is a feature of prophets and noblemen. Yusuf (peace be upon him) always remembered his parents with good while in prison.

﴿وَٱتَّبَعْتُ مِلَّةَ ءَابَآءِى إِبْرَٰهِيمَ وَإِسْحَٰقَ وَيَعْقُوبَ مَا كَانَ لَنَآ أَن نُّشْرِكَ بِٱللَّهِ مِن شَىْءٍ ذَٰلِكَ مِن فَضْلِ ٱللَّهِ عَلَيْنَا وَعَلَى ٱلنَّاسِ وَلَٰكِنَّ أَكْثَرَ ٱلنَّاسِ لَا يَشْكُرُونَ ۝﴾

"I follow the faith of my fathers: Ibrahim, Isaac, and Jacob. It is not ʾrightʿ for us to associate anything with Allah (swt) ʾin worship ʿ. This is part of Allah's grace upon us and humanity, but most people are not grateful"

[TMQ Yusuf – 38]

Ismail (peace be upon him) was an example of righteousness, sacrifice, and surrendering to the order of Allah (swt) and an obedient son to his father

﴿..قَالَ يَٰٓأَبَتِ ٱفْعَلْ مَا تُؤْمَرُ سَتَجِدُنِىٓ إِن شَآءَ ٱللَّهُ مِنَ ٱلصَّٰبِرِينَ ۝﴾

."O my dear father! Do as you are commanded. Allah (swt) willing, you will find me steadfast." [TMQ As-Saffat – 102]

The righteous people still remember their parents with good, treat them well, make charity in their name, and pray for them. All these are the benefits of good *Tarbiyyah* (Nurturing) that sharpen the determinations and help in (being) steadfast.

5. **Destructing and Breaking down the Projects of Westernization and Intellectual Invasion of the Thresholds of _Tarbiyyah_ (Nurturing):**

There is no doubt about the hostility among non-Muslims towards Muslims. Allah (swt) says:

﴿إِن يَثْقَفُوكُمْ يَكُونُوا۟ لَكُمْ أَعْدَآءً وَيَبْسُطُوٓا۟ إِلَيْكُمْ أَيْدِيَهُمْ وَأَلْسِنَتَهُم بِٱلسُّوٓءِ وَوَدُّوا۟ لَوْ تَكْفُرُونَ ۝﴾

"If they gain the upper hand over you, they would be your ˹open˺ enemies, unleashing their hands and tongues to harm you, and wishing that you would abandon faith" [TMQ Al-Mumtahanah – 2]

He further says:

﴿.. قَدْ بَدَتِ ٱلْبَغْضَآءُ مِنْ أَفْوَٰهِهِمْ وَمَا تُخْفِى صُدُورُهُمْ أَكْبَرُ ۝ ..﴾

"Their prejudice has become evident from what they say—and what their hearts hide is far worse" [TMQ Ali-'Imran – 118]

He also says:

﴿وَلَن تَرْضَىٰ عَنكَ ٱلْيَهُودُ وَلَا ٱلنَّصَٰرَىٰ حَتَّىٰ تَتَّبِعَ مِلَّتَهُمْ قُلْ إِنَّ هُدَى ٱللَّهِ هُوَ ٱلْهُدَىٰ ۝ ..﴾

"Never will the Jews or Christians be pleased with you, until you follow their faith. Say, "Allah's guidance is the only ˹true˺ guidance"

[TMQ Al-Baqarah – 120]

There is also no doubt about the people who attribute themselves to Islam in public and express animosity and hatred (towards Islam) in private like Munafiqin (hypocrites) and the people of evil sects and doctrines. Allah (swt) says about the Munafiqin:

$$\text{﴿ .. هُمُ ٱلۡعَدُوُّ فَٱحۡذَرۡهُمۡ ..﴾ ٤}$$

"They are the enemy, so beware of them"   [TMQ Al-Munafiqun – 4}

Today's reality is witnessing a diverse western invasion. It is targeting Muslim homes and is focusing on male and female adolescents. The important thing that can defend against this (western invasion) is to fortify the homes with *Tarbiyyah* (Nurturing) and give preventive doses to the spouse and children. The reality also testifies to the fact that whenever the right *Tarbiyyah* (Nurturing) was made available in the homes, the effects of the invasion have been minimal and vice versa; when the *Tarbiyyah* (Nurturing) is poor, you will see that these invasive waves find their way inside homes easily and conveniently.

Here we must tighten the *Tarbiyyah* (Nurturing), so the projects of secularism and westernization break down when reaching the thresholds of the homes. Male and female *Murabbi's* (nurturers) must fortify and enlighten their homes from the inward and outward infiltration.

We should reflect upon how the Prophet (Peace be upon him) protected, as the first *Murabbi* (Nurturer), his companions from the outside influences. When the Prophet (Peace be upon him) saw Umar carrying a piece of Torah and looking upon it, he (Peace be upon him) stopped him and said:

أمتهوكون فيها يا ابن الخطاب

"Are you confused, O son of Khattab."[154]

It is the awareness of the danger (posed by) the incoming cultures and forbidding from just getting closer to the deviant thoughts.

Indeed, the correct *Tarbiyyah* (Nurturing) in homes firms up the meaning of allegiance to the true religion and values. It resists all forms of subjection and irrational imitation. Therefore, we should pay heed to *Tarbiyyah* (Nurturing) our homes so that the invasive projects of westernization and secularism are destroyed at their door steps.

6. Assisting In Inviting Kin And Relatives (Towards Good):

Calling one's kin and clan towards good and warning them against evil has been mentioned in the texts of the Qur'an and Hadith. There are many examples in the Sirah (biography) of the Prophet (Peace be upon him). He (Peace be upon him) was commanded to invite his close relatives. Allah (swt) says:

﴿وَأَنذِرْ عَشِيرَتَكَ ٱلْأَقْرَبِينَ ٢١٤﴾

"And warn ˈall, starting with ˈyour closest relatives "

[TMQ Ash-Shu'ara – 214]

---

[154] Transmitted by Ibn Abi Shaibah (h/26421), Ahmad (h/15156), al-Darmi (h/449), and al-Bayhaqi in al-Shab (h/175). Albani graded its chain of narration as "strong" in Irwa' al-Ghalil (6/34).

The responsibility and the proclamation (of the message) by the Prophet (Peace be upon him) to Ummah and the commonality of his message to both jinn and humans

$$\langle\text{وَمَآ أَرْسَلْنَـٰكَ إِلَّا كَآفَّةً لِّلنَّاسِ بَشِيرًا وَنَذِيرًا ..}(٢٨)\rangle$$

"We have sent you ˈO Prophetˈ only as a deliverer of good news and a warner to all of humanity"   [TMQ Saba – 28]

didn't hinder or contradict with his call that he made to his close relatives. The Prophet (Peace be upon him) followed the command to deliver the message and call the relatives and the tribesmen (towards Islam) with his *Sahaba* (may Allah (swt) be pleased with them). Abu Dhar was the first who embraced Islam and whom Prophet (Peace be upon him) ordered to go back to his tribe in order to inform them and call them towards Islam.[155]

Abu Dhar (may Allah (swt) be pleased with him) complied with this order, and half of the Ghifar tribe accepted Islam, while the remaining half completed their Islam after meeting the Prophet (Peace be upon him). The Ghifar tribe accepting Islam also led to another tribe (Aslam) embracing Islam. The Prophet (Peace be upon him) said:

غفار غفر الله لها وأسلم سالمها الله

"Allah (swt) forgive the tribes of Ghifar and save the tribes of Aslam."[156]

---

[155] Narrated by Bukhari (h/3861) and Muslim (h/2474).
[156] Bukhari (h/1006) and Muslim (h/675) without mentioning the Shahid.

The same happened with (Tufail bin Amr al-Dausi – may Allah (swt) be pleased with him), who went back to his people as commanded by the Prophet (Peace be upon him) and warned his people and invited them towards Islam. He kept inviting them and treating their mistakes while kept visiting the Prophet (Peace be upon him), asking to pray for them or against them until the tribe (Daus) accepted Islam with the supplication of the Prophet (Peace be upon him): "O Allah! Give guidance to the Daus (tribe) and bring them (to Islam)!"[157]

Inviting kin and relatives (towards good) has become easy in our times, and there is a strong need for that. However, what is regrettable is the weak participation of the good people and students. Their presence is like others without any positive impact, except those upon whom Allah (swt) showers his mercy. Homes being filled in terms of knowledge, *Da'wah* (calling towards Islam), and *Tarbiyyah* (Nurturing) increase the effectiveness of inviting close relatives. This goodness and *Da'wah* flows to other homes of relatives as these families that have taken their share of *Tarbiyyah* (Nurturing) feel their positive role with their bigger clan, and they take the initiative to provide beneficial programs to the family.

How can a family that is negligent in its own *Tarbiyyah* (Nurturing) and *Da'wah* assist other families, while she itself is in need of the *Da'wah* and *Tarbiyyah* over others?

Assisting in calling (*Da'wah*) the kin and close relatives, offering good, and warning from evil has become necessary in this time of invasion and capture of the Family. The need for it gets stronger

---

[157] Buhkari (h/4392) and Muslim (h/2524).

with the challenges of (secularism) and the (Muslim home) being the target.

It has become necessary to *Tarbiyyah* (Nurture) our homes for good, so they become a starting point in assisting in (the process of *Da'wah*) inviting relatives and tribesmen. This is one of the benefits of paying attention to homes and educating the household members on positive participation. So, are we ready to do that?

Sources and References

1. Al-Qur'an al-Karim

2. Sahih al-Bukhari (al-Jami' al-Sahih): Mohammad bin Ismail al-Bukhari (d. 256h)

3. Sahih Muslim: Investigation by Mohammad Fu'ad Abdul Baqi, Published by: Presidency of Scientific Research, Ifta', *Da'wah*, and Guidance, Kingdom of Saudi Arabia (1400H)

4. Sahih al-Jami' al-Saghir and Additions: Mohammad Nasir al-Din al-Albani, Published by: al-Maktab al-Islami

5. Tafsir al-Tabri: Abu Ja'far Mohammad bin Jari al-Tabri (d.310 h). Ma'rfiah Printing and Publishing House, Beirut

6. al-Jami' li Ahkam al-Qur'an: Abu Abdullah Mohammad bin Ahmad al-Qurtubi (d.671h). Third Edition (Dar al-Kutub, Cairo 1387h)

7. Tafsir al-Qur'an al-Azim: Abu al-Fida' Ismail bin Umar bin Kathir (d. 774h.), Investigation: Abdul Aziz Ghaneem, Mohammad Ahmad Ashur, Mohmmad Ibrahim al-Banna, Dar al-Sha'b Printing, Cairo.

8. al-Buyut fi al-Qur'an al-Karim by Sa'doon Jum'a al-Halboos, published by Dar al-Zaman, First Edition 1424h.

9. Siyar a'lam an-Nubala, Mohammad bin Ahmad bin Uthman al-Dhahbi (d.748), Research supervised by Shuaib al-Arna'ot, who also extracted its *Ahadith*. A number of people carried Investigation on the book, including Husain al-Asad, Saleh al-Simar, Published by al-Risalah Foundation, First Edition (1401).

10. Al-Sirah al-Nabawiyah: Mohammad bin Ahmad bin Uthman al-Dhahbi (d.748). Text Investigation and Footnotes Writing by Husam al-Din al-Maqdasi, Published by Dar Maktabah al-Hilal, Beirut

11. al-Tabqat al-Kubra: Muḥammad ibn Sa'd ibn Mani' al-Basri al-Zuhri (d. 230h), Published by: Dar Sadir, Beirut.

12. Al-Musnad: Imam Ahmad bin Hanbal (d.241h), Investigation: Ahmad Shakir, Published by: Dar Sadir, al-Maktab al-Islami.

13. Mukhtasar Sahih Muslim: al-Hafiz al-Munzari (Zaki al-Din Abdul Azeem), Investigation: Mohammad Nasir al-Din al-Albani, Published by: al-Maktab al-Islami / Beirut, Third Edition 1397h.

14. Fathul Bari: Ahmad bin Ali bin Hajar al-Asqalani (d.852), His books, chapters, discussions were numbered and footnotes explored by: Mohammed Fouad Abdel Bari. Edited and Supervised by: Moheb al-Din Al-Khatib: Publication and Distribution: Presidency of Scientific Research and Fatwas Departments. Kingdom of Saudi Arabia.

15. al-Isaba fi Tamyiz al-*Sahaba*: Ahmed bin Ali bin Hajar Al-Asqalani (T852 H), Investigation by Dr. Taha Mohammed Al-Zaini, Published: Library of Al-Azhar Colleges in Al-Azhar, first edition (1396 AH).

16. Sunan Abi Dawood: Sule*Iman* ibn Al-Ashaith, Published by: Scientific Council for the Revival of Islamic Heritage, Fist Edition,1406 AH/1986.

17. Saheeh Sunan Abi Dawood: Mohammed Nasser al-Din al-Albani, Published by: Arab Education Office for the Gulf States/Riyadh, First Edition, 1409 AH/1988.

18. Jami al-Usool fi *Ahadith* al-Rasul: Ibn Al-Athir al-Jazri (d. 606 AH), Investigation: Abdul Qader al-Arnaout, Published by: Halwani Library, Al-MAllah (swt) Press, Dar Al Bayan Library (1389 AH).

19. Zad al-Ma'ad fi Hadyi Khairil Ibad: Ibn Al-Qayyim: Abu Abdullah Mohammed bin Abi Bakr bin Qayyim al-Jouzia (d. 51 AH), Investigation by: Shuaib al-Arnaout, and Abdul Qader al-Arnaout, Published by: Resala Foundation, Al-Manar Islamic Library, First Edition (1399 AH).

20. Sharh us-Sunnah: Abu Mohammed Al-Hussein bin Masoud bin Mohammed Al-Baghwi (d.516 AH), Investigation: Shuaib al-Arnaout - Mohammed Zuhair Aa-Shawaish, Publisher: Islamic Office, Damascus, Beirut, Second Edition, 1403H/1983.

21. Ahkam al-Qur'an: Emad al-Din bin Mohammed al-Tabari (Al-Kia Al-Harasi, 504 AH), Investigation: Mousa Mohammed Ali, and Izza Ali Eid Attiyah, Published by: Modern Books House/Egypt.

22. Irwa al-Ghalil fi Takhrij al-Hadith Manar al-Sabil: Mohammed Nasir al-Din al-Albani, Published by: Islamic Office/Beirut, First Edition, 1399 AH.

23. Sahih al-Adab al-Mufrad: (Imam Bukhari) Investigation: Muhammad Nassir Al-Din Al-Albani, Second Edition, 1415 AH, Published by: Dar al-Sadiq/Jubail: Saudi Arabia.

24. The components of the Happy Home: Mohammed bin Abdulrahman Al-Zeer, First Edition, 1439 AH.

25. Forty Tips for Reforming Homes: Mohammed bin Saleh Al-Munjid, First Edition, 1436H/2015, Published by: Zaad Publishing Group.

26. The Etiquette of Treating (others) in the Prophetic Biography: Dr. SuleIman bin Hamad Al-Awda, First Edition,1428 AH, Published by: Al-Diya' Charity House, Buraidah.

27. Angels Do Not Enter These Houses: Ibrahim Al-Jamal, Published by: Endowment Library, in front of the Green Door/ Sayyidina Al-Hussein.

28. The Authentic Biography and the Prophet's Guidance in the Books of Sunnah: First Edition, 1437 AH. Published by: Sheikh Abdullah Al-Rashid Chair to serve the biography and the Messenger Peace be upon him /Qassim University.

29. The Acronym of True Prophetic Biography: Dr. SuleIman bin Hamad Al-Awda, First Edition 1440H, Published by: Bayan Message House for Publication and Distribution.

30. Provisions and Etiquette of Entering Homes: Dr. Abdul Karim bin Yousef Al-Khadar, First Edition 1439 AH

31. Encyclopedia of Authentic *Ahadith* containing the Prophetic Feautures: Dr. Humam Abdulrahman Saeed and his son, Published by: Bayan Magazine /Riyadh, First Edition: 1432 AH.